NAS

A Parish ...ory

Edited by

R. L. GREENALL

Department of Adult Education
University of Leicester
1974

CONTENTS

ILLUSTRATIONS, MAPS, AND TABLES

INTRODUCTION

This publication is the result of work done by students on a local history course in Naseby in the winter of 1972-73 promoted by the Adult Education Department of Leicester University.

The object has been to produce an account of the history of the parish and its people aimed at the ordinary reader or visitor to Naseby. It was not intended to attempt a balanced history doing justice to all periods because the source materials for such a work simply have not survived. Nevertheless using such evidence as early parish registers, the log books of the village school, the Methodist Chapel records, and wills and probate inventories — all particularly useful for group work — Bridges' *History and Antiquities of Northamptonshire* (1791), the Rev. John Mastin's *History and Antiquities of Naseby* (1792), and miscellaneous documents in record offices, it has been possible to produce a narrative of Naseby's long history.

Almost all previous historical writing on Naseby has been dominated by the battle so in this work an effort has been made to relegate that momentous event to the place of an episode which chanced to take place in the parish. Yet though it was felt that the work should be concerned more with the people of Naseby than the battle, it would have been absurd to ignore it altogether. Hence in the pages which follow there is an account of that important action in 1645.

Although this is an account of Naseby's history designed for the general reader rather than the specialist, it has been largely built up from primary source material, and it would have been slipshod to have excluded references to this material where they need to be made. Many of these have been made inside the text, and, though footnotes on the page have been excluded, a list of additional references may be found at the end of the book.

The following people were the members of the course. All worked on the basic source material and provided the first accounts on which the narrative is based: R. E. Beck, Mr. and Mrs. R. M. Bird, (Mrs.) E. M. Bromell, D. L. Hackett, Mr. and Mrs. M. S. Hallworth, Mr. and Mrs. M. J. Hayward, C. Hill, Mr. and Mrs. R. Jeffries, the Rev. and Mrs. J. W. S. Mansell, Mr. and Mrs. A. McKendrick, Mr. and Mrs. E. H. Westaway, Mr. and Mrs. M. Westaway, (Mrs.) M. Westaway, and (Mrs.) P. E. Worlledge.

The group wish to thank the Archivists and staffs of the Northampton-shire and the Ipswich and East Suffolk Record Offices for their help in locating maps and documentary sources, Northampton public library, the University of Cambridge Committee for Aerial Photography for permission to reproduce Dr. St. Joseph's air photograph of the village, Mr. S. Brookes for the loan of the school log books, the Rev. John Mansell and the parish council for the use of parish records, and the Rev. Victor Martin of Market Harborough for the use of papers relating to the Methodist Chapel.

The University Centre
Northampton.

Part I   Naseby in 1973

Naseby, as every schoolboy knows, is the Northamptonshire parish in which the decisive battle between King and Parliament in the Civil War was fought in 1645. It lies thirteen miles north of Northampton, close to the borders with Warwickshire and Leicestershire. In appearance it is a typical open-field parish of the English midlands; the nucleated village with its fine church and spire stands centrally on high ground surrounded by its extensive fields. There is, however, something different about Naseby. Though of the midland plain, it is an upland village; even today it stands remote. Naseby is on a watershed; not only the watershed of Northamptonshire, but on that of the very midlands. At the north end of the village rises the 'Warwickshire' Avon, flowing westwards to the Severn and the Bristol Channel; at the south end the northern tributary of the Nene rises, flowing first south to Northampton, thence north-east to the Wash. Naseby has four other streams, and every one of them flows out of the parish. It is the principal high place of Northamptonshire. From the top of the church tower the churches of forty parishes have been counted, and, so it is said, on days of exceptional clarity the glint of the North Sea in the Wash has been seen. The words of Thomas Carlyle, Cromwell's biographer, written a hundred and thirty years or so ago capture the main features of its topography: "the grounds . . . lie high . . . the hills are broad blunt clayey masses, swelling toward and from each other like indolent waves of a sea, sometimes of miles in extent".[1] The soil is almost entirely red Liassic clay and boulder clay: though cold, it is good land for crops, even better for grazing.

Naseby today is beginning to climb away from one of its lowest points in population. A steady decline for more than a century to about 350 inhabitants is now being reversed by the selling-off of land in the village for house building, and the population is pushing up again towards 400. There are the village institutions one would expect to find — Parish Church and Methodist Chapel, British Legion, Women's Institute, cricket club, and Old People's club. Two pubs, the *Fitzgerald Arms* and the *Royal Oak,* serve more than the local needs of the village and bring people out from the towns. The old village National school still accommodates the five to eleven year olds, but is now run by the local authority, the church appointing certain of the managers only. For their secondary education the children go to the comprehensive school at Guilsborough.

What separates modern Naseby from its past is that it is no longer mainly a farming community. Apart from the farmers and their immediate families only a dozen or so men today work on the land. The two businesses in the village — a garage and a fencing contractor — by no means absorb the village's labour force. The majority of the working population is employed outside Naseby — as railway workers, lorry drivers, factory workers, and council employees, or are professional men or business executives. Nearly all work in Market Harborough or Northampton. The number of farms in the parish has remained constant over the last hundred years, but in these days a farmer is not easily defined: some have only

1

small farms and follow other occupations as well; others specialise in pigs or poultry and have no land other than that on which their buildings stand; in yet other instances two or more farms might belong to the same family and be farmed either together or as separate businesses. In this area, once famous for its pastures, arable farming now predominates, although most farms still have some sheep and beef cattle. But there are now only three dairy herds in the village and even the 'house cow' is something that has virtually disappeared.

Naseby is a shrunken village. All recent building has been within the historic framework of roads and streets — the map of the village in 1973 differs remarkably little from the earliest surviving map, drawn in 1630. Naseby's foundations are underneath its modern surface. The history of the place is what this book is about.

Part II Naseby before 1792

From its origins to Domesday

Naseby is an ancient site of settlement, and its antiquity is almost certainly explained by its geographical position. Professor Grimes in his essay on the Jurassic Way — that major prehistoric route which ran across England from the Humber to the Mendips, entering Northamptonshire at Stamford and following the uplands to Banbury — has suggested that one of the paths of the Way went *via* Naseby to Daventry, and thence to Edgehill.[2] Naseby's watershed position is thus an important one. But so far, archaeological evidence of Naseby's antiquity has not been abundant. Recent field-walking has produced some examples of worked flint and one fine flint axe. In the 1870s the Reverend Assheton Pownall exhibited a 'celt of bronze' found on the Naseby Woolleys estate by a labourer employed in drainage work. One end was chisel shaped; the other terminated as a small adze. Recent photographs taken from the air reveal crop marks showing concentric circular enclosures in a field north of the village which may well date from the bronze age or iron age; though at ground level there is no trace of them. In 1874 a Roman urn found in draining operations contained 38 silver *denarii* dated from the time of Vespasian to Aurelius (69 A.D. to 180 A.D.). In 1924 another hoard of Roman coins was found in the area of Naseby Woolleys. But so far, however, no archaeological evidence has been found of a Roman villa or other pre-Saxon settlement in the parish.

At first glance the place-name Naseby might seem to be obviously Scandinavian in origin, like those of its immediate neighbours, Cold Ashby or Sulby. However, its origin is *Hnaefes-burh* or possibly *Hnaefes-byrig* (the

2

fortified place of one *Hnaef*). Hnaef is a very early Old English name, recorded in the heroic poetry of the West Germanic tribes, but not appearing anywhere else in the Anglian settlement of this country except in one reference in a Hampshire charter.[3] Its place-name therefore suggests Naseby was not a Scandinavian settlement of the ninth or tenth century A.D. but an early Saxon settlement probably of the sixth century. Another point about Naseby as an early settlement is that it is (apart from Guilsborough) the only one in a district which was apparently empty of English villages until the Danish settlement — which produced Holdenby, Ravensthorpe, Cold Ashby, Thornby, and Sulby. These villages are of course on the Northampton uplands, their soil is heavy, and it seems likely that they would be colonized by later rather than early waves of settlers. Probably Naseby was an early settlement because of its strategic position on the watershed. In addition, it has been suggested that the founding of Naseby may not have been part of the Anglian colonization of Northamptonshire, which followed the route of the Nene valley from the east, at all. It is possible (arguing from the fact that there is archaeological evidence revealing very early settlements in the south east part of the country) Naseby might have been the most northerly outpost of a colonizing push by Saxons from the upper Thames Valley *via* Daventry.[4] But from archaeological finds the only evidence of Saxon Naseby which has been discovered to date is a trefoil-headed brooch found in the late 19th century, which is now in the British Museum.

Of the Danish period we have little evidence. *Hnaefesburh* had by 1086 become *Navesberie*, which is the oldest recorded spelling of the name we have. (As late as 1700 Naseby was being spelt *Navesby*). It is just possible that the south-western part of the village, Nutcote, may have originated as a Danish suburb added to the Saxon village. Writing in 1792 the Reverend John Mastin spelt it *Knutcoat*, but that may have been a piece of unconscious antiquarianism on his part, because it was *Nutcote* on the map of 1630. It seems much more likely that Nutcote was added to Naseby not in the Anglo-Saxon period but in the middle ages.

Domesday Book gives us the first documentary picture of Naseby. It tells us that in 1086 the lord of the manor of Naseby was now William Peveril. For his part in the conquest Peveril was given (in Northamptonshire alone) manors in the Higham Ferrers district and near Naseby — Clipston, Nobottle, Althorp, Brington, Harlestone, Flore and Duston. On the subject of who the last Anglo-Saxon lord of Naseby was Domesday Book is silent. But it does tell us that its value had increased from 20 shillings in 1066 to 60 shillings in 1086, Naseby having been laid waste in 1065 by the Northumbrian and Welsh supporters of Earl Morcar who had overthrown Tostig and had marched south on Northampton. By 1086 the population had recovered to a total of perhaps 105 or so people, Domesday listing 21 tenants, probably heads of families (two socmen, eight villeins and eleven bordars), together with a priest. The survey tells us (less usefully) that the manor was assessed for Geld at seven hides, that there were fourteen 'ploughlands', that there were two plough teams for the lord's demesne (or farm) and that the villeins had three ploughs between them. There were, it said, eight acres of meadow.

Naseby in the Middle Ages

From the time of William the Conqueror until the thirteenth year of the reign of Henry VIII, Naseby belonged to a succession of great barons whose main estates were outside Northamptonshire. From William Peveril it passed into the hands of another French family, the Seigneurs of Laval, all of whom were called Guy de Laval, who held it for most of the twelfth century. When Guy VII lost his English lands in 1199 Naseby passed into the possession of the crusader, Roger de Lacey, Constable of Chester.

Under Guy VII the first of a series of charters granting land in Naseby to the Abbey of Sulby (founded in 1155) began, and grants to Sulby continued until the early fourteenth century, so that perhaps as much as a third of the parish of Naseby was, by the time of Henry VIII part of the estates of the Abbey.[5] In 1203 or 1204 Roger de Lacey secured for his newly acquired manor a charter granting Naseby a weekly market. It was at this time that the street at the top of the village called Newland was probably laid out and a market cross opposite the north door of the church erected. How long Naseby remained a market town we do not know for certain. But it is likely that it was about 150 to 200 years, during the years of medieval expansion in the thirteenth century, and into the fourteenth. The shaft of the last market cross still stands in the village.

For a generation, Naseby remained a manor of the de Laceys and then passed to Richard de Clare, Earl of Gloucester and Hereford through his marriage with Maud de Lacey. In 1238, the year in which he took part in the notorious tournament at Brackley, Richard had thirty oak trees delivered to him at Naseby from the forest of Geddington.[6] It would seem likely that these were used to facilitate some fairly large building project at Naseby possibly a manor house, or some houses for new tenants, because the village was certainly growing in size at this time.

The manor stayed in the possession of the Earls of Gloucester and Hereford until 1316 when Gilbert de Clare was slain fighting the Scots at Bannockburn, and for want of male heirs his inheritance passed to his three sisters. Naseby passed to the second sister, Margaret, who married Hugh de Audele, Baron of Stafford, on whom the manor was settled for his lifetime by the King. This manor Hugh held of the King by service of a single rose yearly at Midsummer.[7] The Earls of Stafford in their turn granted the manor to under-tenants. In 1318, for instance, John Gifford was certified as lord of Naseby, and in 1347 the manors of Rothwell, Naseby (*Navesby*), Whiston and Glapthorn were held by John de Gynewell, canon of the church of St. Mary, Salisbury, and Master Ralph de Gadesbury.[8] The canon of Sarum left his name in Naseby; to this day one of the streets is called Gynwell.

The manor remained in the possession of the Stafford family for more than a hundred and seventy years until 1499 when the last of them, who by then held the title of Earl of Wiltshire, died without issue and the manor passed to a relative, Edward Duke of Buckingham. In 1521 Buckingham incurred the wrath of Henry VIII and was beheaded for treason, and his manor of Naseby was granted to an opulent London alderman, Sir William Fitzwilliam, the founder of the family of Fitzwilliam of Milton.

NASEBY ABOUT 1790

An engraving by Samuel Ireland. It shows the spring from which the River Avon rises (now in the garden of Manor Farm), the Parish Church, and the medieval market place and market cross in Newland. This scene had probably not changed much since the Middle Ages. When working up his sketch Ireland washed in the outline of the iron supports of the copper ball on the incompleted spire — giving a misleading impression of the stump and ball.

The account of the descent of the Lordship from the time of the Conqueror to Henry VIII does not tell us a lot about Naseby itself. However, certain things are clear. Possibly because it was merely part of the considerable possessions of mighty but distant lords, the manor and the estate were not separated. In a list of the Earl of Wiltshire's English lands dating from the 1490s Naseby was the single most valuable of them all, indicating that there was a big land holding there as well as the dues of the manor.[9] It seems that when Sir William Fitzwilliam acquired the lordship of Naseby he also acquired some two thirds of the land of the parish as well — about 2,000 acres. No doubt closely connected with this was another fact of importance: in the later middle ages land tenure in Naseby had become entirely leasehold. There were no freeholders or copyholders. Naseby was thus a 'closed village' dominated by the owners of the two large estates, or their stewards.

5

In the middle ages Naseby probably followed the pattern of midland parishes in that there was a steady expansion of population and land under the plough until the early fourteenth century, the granting of the market charter in 1203 or 1204 no doubt stimulating growth. From the early fourteenth century the population declined, especially after the Great Pestilence of 1349. Some idea of the size of the population in the generation after the Plague can be obtained from the poll tax receipt of 1377. This reveals that Naseby paid 54 shillings and four pence, which gives a figure of 163 people paying the tax of four pence per head, excluding children, religious, and mendicants.[10] If we allow a calculation of forty per cent for them, we have a figure of about 270 or so for the population in 1377. And; if we follow Professor Russell's calculation that the population in 1377 in Midland England was about sixty *per cent* of what it had been at its peak, before the so-called Black Death,[11] this would give a figure of 450 for Naseby at the height of the Middle Ages. If this is correct, it was a population that Naseby was not to reach again until about the year 1670.

Another source of information about the plague of 1349 is given by Professor Shrewsbury in his *History of the Bubonic Plague in the British Isles.* Analysing mortality among the beneficed clergy in the Northampton-shire deaneries he calculated that in the deanery of Daventry 30% of the parish priests died in 1349; in Rothwell 43%; in Northampton 38%; and in East Haddon, the deanery Naseby was in, 36%. It seems clear that Simon of Anderby (the priest of Naseby since 1341) died of the plague, for his successor Nicholas of Croxale was instituted rector on 13 July 1349, when the contagion was at its height. Further evidence for a shrinkage of the population in later medieval Naseby comes from comparing the air photograph taken by Dr. St. Joseph with the plan of the village taken from the map of 1630. The air photograph shows unmistakably that Nutcote had once had cottages with gardens and orchards, and that these had been abondoned, and not subsequently ploughed up, whilst the map shows that in 1630 these houses and gardens had apparently vanished completely. The most likely conclusion is that this part of the village had been depopulated in the later fourteenth or fifteenth century.

The Medieval Church in Naseby

Christianity probably first reached Naseby from the minster church at Brixworth late in the seventh or in the eighth century A.D. No information about the first five hundred years of Christianity in the parish survives, though some Saxon stones are apparently built into the walls of the present church, and there is an incised grave slab in the wall in the tower. Domesday Book mentions a priest, but not a church, though one probably existed. Possibly it was enlarged in Norman times; the font survives from this period.

The earliest parts of the present church of All Saints date from the thirteenth century, the years after the granting of the market charter; the south aisle, pillars and wall (but not the windows) from about 1220-

AIR PHOTOGRAPH OF NASEBY FROM THE SOUTH WEST

Showing the abandoned medieval house sites with their gardens and orchards, the hollows of water-courses, and possibly two small fish ponds in the centre of the photograph. Compare with map of the village in 1630. (Photograph *Cambridge University Collection: copyright reserved*.)

1240, and the north aisle from about 1280. The clerestory above the arches on both sides of the church, and the upper part of the tower and the lower part of the spire were built about 1400. The spire was left an uncompleted stump by the fifteenth century builders, but in the eighteenth century George Ashby, the patron of the living, caused a curious addition to be made to it in the form of a king post and four supports on top of which a large copper ball was mounted, topped by a weather vane. According to Naseby's historian, the Rev. John Mastin, this ball was loot from Boulogne, brought home in 1544 by Sir Gyles Allington and placed

7

on the cupola of his house at Horseheath in Cambridgeshire. It was bought by Mr. Ashby 'for its weight, as old copper', and mounted on the church stump of Naseby. Today it stands in the churchyard, the spire having been completed in the church restoration of 1860, and the incongruous copper ball removed.

Until the year 1430 Naseby was a rectory, but in that year Humphrey, Earl of Stafford, the patron and lord of the manor, gave the living to the Abbey of Combe in Warwickshire. The Abbot of Combe then secured the permission of the Bishop of Lincoln to impropriate the rectory, that is, to annex its income. Before permitting this the Bishop arranged that the Abbey should appoint a priest to reside in the parish, and that he should have a fixed stipend out of the living. For the next hundred years, until the Abbey was dissolved by Henry VIII in 1539 the vicars of Naseby were usually monks of Combe. In that year the patronage of Naseby and the rights to the Naseby glebe were granted to Mary, Duchess of Richmond, who later sold them to John Shuckburgh, who became patron and lay rector.

The long history of catholic Naseby is largely lost but we can learn a little about religion in the generation before the Reformation from bequests to the parish church of All Hallows made in wills of Naseby people of that time.[12] In the church there were a number of lights, images and altars. We find John Walche in 1512 leaving a rod of peas, and William Collis in 1529 one 'wether hoggrell' [a castrated yearling sheep] to Our Lady Light in the Chancel; William Hawforth in 1530 leaving two sheep to Our Lady of Pity Light; John Walshe in 1512 a 'stryke [sheaf] of barley' to Our Lady of Grace; John Ysott 'to the cherche of Navysbe vjs.viijd. to by candystykes in the rode loft' in 1523; and so on. In their wills Naseby men and women also left bequests to buy vestments, church plate, new bells, and to maintain and repair the church. Thus Thomas Palmer in 1529 left 12 pence 'to helpe to by a cope'; John Ysott in 1523 'vjs.viijd. towarde a new chasuble'; Alice Belhost in 1529 'to the bying of a challyce or a forebell xs; Richard Adam de Isledon in 1474 12 pence to buy two cruets of pewter; Henry Belhost 20 shillings to buy a 'grayle' [graduale or service book] in 1523; Richard Bunche 10 shillings towards a new bell in 1529; and Thomas Hawford eight pence to the repair of the south aisle in 1536.

They left donations for their 'mortuaries' [customary gifts to the priest from their estate], regulations about their funerals and directions for special masses. Thus for his 'corse present' [or mortuary] Thomas Cosbie in 1529 left the priest his 'best horse' and in the same year Thomas Jeffare bequeathed him a hen, 18 chickens and six cheeses. For his funeral in 1529 Myles Roos left most elaborate directions: 'I wyle that there be ij blake clothes with white crosses on my grave and on my wyvis, & ther on to be sett ij sergis [cierges, large wax candles] to bren [burn] att all masses that shall be sayd for me and my wyve, and all massis at the hy auter [altar] during one yere. Item every person that shall be att my beryall shall have ijd. Also I wyll that every house in the town shall have a chese, & the porest house the best chese'.

Tudor and Stuart Naseby

What happened in Naseby at the time of the Reformation in the 1530s is by no means clear. From the wills we get some intimations. We first notice that the name of the church was 'protestantized' from All Hallows to All Saints (its present dedication), in the will of Richard Morton (1554). Before the Reformation it was customary for people making their wills to bequeath two pence or so to the 'mother church' at Lincoln. From 1541 this practice was kept up except that the bequests were to the cathedral of the new diocese in which Northamptonshire now found itself; so in 1543 William Fypp left four pence to 'the mother church at peterborowe'. It is noticeable that from about 1540 bequests are more directed towards the relief of poverty than hitherto, though this no doubt reflects the growth of poverty as the population began to increase as much as a more charitable urge as a result of the Reformation. We find Thomas Halforde directing in 1541 that every house in Naseby should have a penny worth of bread, and that twenty of them (presumably the poorest) 'a peny a peece more', William Aspland in 1572 leaving a similar payment to every 'poore householder cawled a cottyar', and Edward Goosey in 1608 leaving 'to everie poore household not having either land or bakehouse ij*d* a house in bread'.

An important result of the Reformation for Naseby was that much of the land of the parish changed hands as a result of the dissolution of the Abbey of Sulby. Bridges tells us that in 1545 'Navesby Grange and other lands here were given to George Rithe [?Riche] and Thomas Grantham', and that 'the convent of Sulby had possessions in Navesby which by the survey in 1535 . . . were valued at xlv*s*.iv*d*. yearly. These with other lands in this neighbourhood were granted in the tenth and twelfth of Queen Elizabeth (1568 and 1570) to Sir Christopher Hatton'. Sometime after 1545 all these monastic lands passed into the hands of the Shuckburgh family, whose descendants down to the late nineteenth century were proprietors of about a third of the parish of Naseby.

An inscription in Naseby church on the tombstone of the last male Shuckburgh (who died in 1658) celebrates 'the antiquitie of his familie which . . . flourished there in a perpetuall descent for many years'. In fact the earliest mention of the family in Naseby is of Thomas Shuckburgh in 1476, but nothing more is known of them for another century when another tombstone in the church records that John Shuckburgh died in 1576 leaving his widow with those surviving children from their family of three sons and thirteen daughters. John was succeeded by his third son Edward (born in 1572). Edward lived to the ripe old age of 86 and it is probably he that brought together the land in Naseby which came to comprise the Shuckburgh inheritance. He was High Sheriff of the county in 1623, and Mastin makes the curious claim that he was the owner of the first waggon in Northamptonshire. He had a tithe barn erected in Naseby (no doubt to hold the tithes due to him as impropriator), a timber of which had his initials 'ES' and the date '1601' inscribed on it. Village tradition has it that he purchased the barn in Norfolk and had brought it to Naseby and had it re-erected. It was demolished shortly after the second world war. His eldest son Eusebie predeceased him, and so his inheritance passed to Eusebie's daughter Mary, who married George Ashby of Quenby Hall, Leicestershire, their son George being baptised in Naseby in 1656. George Ashby, who was twice Member of Parliament, had a very long wait for his Naseby inheritance; his mother lived even longer than her grandfather, not dying until 1721 at the age of ninety-three. She died a Mrs. Hewet, having re-married to a Colonel Hewet of Rotherby, after the death of George Ashby of Quenby. Not a lot is known about this branch of the Shuckburghs, but it is clear that in the years they lived in the village down to 1658 they were the squires of Naseby. Their 'venerable, old, but sombrous seat' (as Mastin described it) stood next to the vicarage in the centre of the village, but was pulled down in 1773 and rebuilt as a farm house, which stands to this day.

The series of a hundred or so surviving Naseby wills and probate inventories of the 16th and 17th centuries throws some light on the economic and social life of the people of the village in this period. The picture they give is that of a community of small tenant farmers and poor cottagers, with only a few families of substance, such as the Wrights, the Simondses, the Gooseys, and later in the 17th century, the Everards.

In the early part of the period Naseby farmers seem largely to have been grain and wool producers. Their wills and inventories mention crops of hay, corn, rye, barley and peas, and virtually all kept sheep, flocks varying from about twenty to forty. It was a poor husbandman indeed in Naseby who could not bequeath to his favourite nephew, grandchild or godchild a lamb or a ewe in his will. Down to the latter part of the 17th century cattle seem very largely to have been for domestic use and few in number; it is only from about 1680 that they seem to have increased in importance in the village economy. Chickens are scarcely mentioned at all, there are few references to pigs, and hives of bees are mentioned only once, in the inventory of John Wilson in 1630. Although none of the farmers were freeholders in Naseby a few owned houses or land in neighbouring parishes. John Crisp in 1635 for instance left his grandson 'half a cottage house' in Clipston, and Jane Wright in 1611 left her son a close of pasture in Kelmarsh field. A most important event in the farming year was the five-day fair at Rothwell which began on Trinity Monday (the week after Whit Monday). There Naseby farmers met kinsfolk and neighbours, redeemed bonds and settled debts.

The wills and inventories give a very clear picture of material possessions and their value. Lists of clothing and household utensils such as tables and chairs, beds and chests, fireplace furniture and cutlery were carefully itemized and bequeathed. The desire for continuity of family possessions so marked in the gentry is found in the humbler classes as well. Thus in 1610 Richard Ward declared 'alsoe my will is that my two sylver spoones, my great brasse pott, my great yron spitt to be kept and remaine as standers to my house with John Warde my sonne, and he to leave them in like manner as they have been given by my elders in tyme past by their wills'.

NASEBY: VILLAGE AND PEOPLE IN 1630 (*opposite*)
Traced from an enlarged photograph of the lord of the manor's estate map of that date in the Fitzgerald papers in the Ipswich and East Suffolk Record Office.

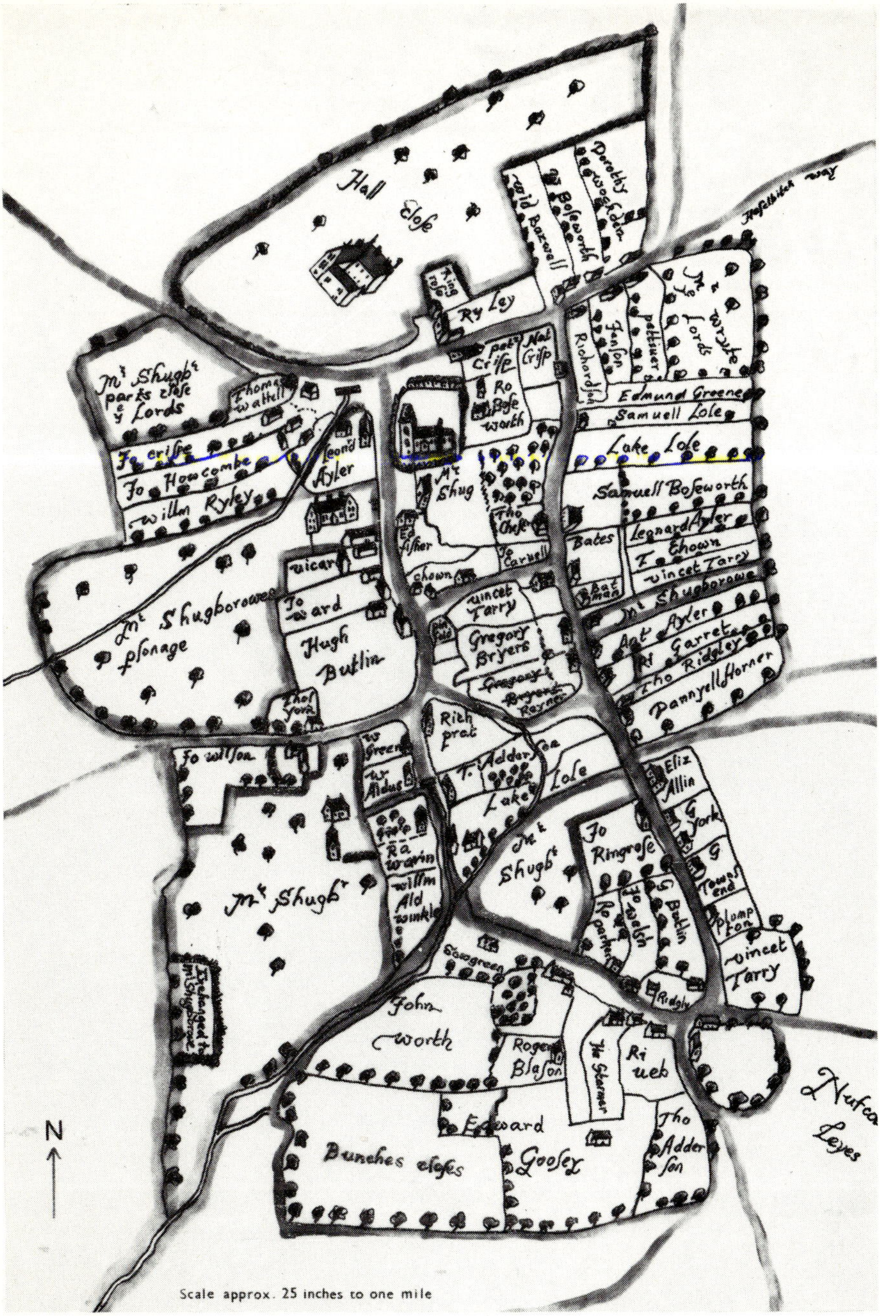

Scale approx. 25 inches to one mile

A major consideration in those days of high mortality was to make provision for children and widows. Robert Prat in 1597 made very careful provision for the material needs of his wife Alice after his decease. His son was to provide 'meate, drinke, lodging, beddings, fyer, rayment, apparel, linnen, woollen hose, shooes, and all other necessarie things meet and convenient for a woman of her callinge', and she was also to have an allowance of sixpence per quarter. He added, however, that if she left the family farm at Naseby and went to live with any of her other children 'then my will is that she shall have vli for her parte, and not anything els and to depart with quietnesse'. Richard Ferrys in 1599 went into detail about what should happen if his widow and their son could not agree — even appointing the overseers of his will umpires in any dispute. And in 1638 William Wilson faced up to a by no means uncommon situation: 'and whereas my wyfe does mistrust her selfe to be with childe but knoweth not certayne whether it be soe or not, if it be soe I doe give to it vili xiijs iiijd. If it be not soe my will is that vjli xiijs iiijd shalbe equally divided amongst the other my three children'. Lawrence Wright (1599) left his widow a half share with their son-in-law Jasper Simonds, and willed that 'they shall occupye the farm together as he and I have done'.

The personal gifts in wills reveal something of other matters which concerned these farmers and their families. Thomas Halford reminds us of the medieval England that was past when in 1541 he left his friend Henry Dunckley his bow. And the wills of Edward Goosey (1608) and of his godson the Reverend Edward Wright (1632) throw light on the intellectual, religious and civic interests of two Naseby families. Edward Goosey was a yeoman farmer and evidently also a schoolmaster. To his godson, the rector of Clipston, he left 'a book at his owne choyce in my slender library, of the Latin books'. To his eldest son Richard Goosey he gave the right to take part of his books and bestow the rest amongst his brothers and sisters, but stipulated that his second son Edward, evidently destined to succeed him as schoolmaster, was to have 'the most and the school books'. To the vicar of Naseby, Richard Coxe (or Cockes) he bequeathed what perhaps was his treasured possession, his 'Exposition of Mr. Calvin upon the Commandments'.

The probate inventory of his godson, the Reverend Edward Wright (1569-1632), rector of Clipston and vicar of Naseby in succession to Richard Coxe (who died in 1611) reveals that he had a library of books valued at £20 and debts of £11 owing to him for the 'dyet and teaching of certain schollers'. He was also a proprietor of substance having forty sheep and three cows in Sibbertoft field, a farm in Naseby, and (clearly marking him as a man of some wealth) thirty shillings worth of pit coals in his vicarage yard. Perhaps more surprising are bequests in his will of 1632 to his successor at Clipston. He left the new incumbent all his right and interest in 'one light horse, and the saddle, bridle and furniture thereto belonging, and allso all my right and interest of and in the armour for the ryder of the said light horse'. He also gave to Mrs. Hawford of East Farndon his part of 'that musket which now she hath in her possession'. These apparently martial interests were in fact the vicar's contribution to the defence of the realm, in the form of equipment for the Northamptonshire Trained Bands, which 'the two Parsons of Clipston' were required to provide and maintain.

It is clear from the wills that there was an obligation on men of some wealth to bear in mind their civic responsibilities to the 'town' of Naseby. Thus in 1534 we find William Fypp leaving three shillings and fourpence to 'the mendynge of the cawsay att calvell townsende'; Richard Morton leaving twelve pence 'towarde amendinge the towns wells' in 1554; Robert Goosey remembering 'Debts which I owe to the towne stocke of Navesbye' in 1556; and Edward Goosey in 1608 leaving three shillings and fourpence to the repair of the Church, highways and wells.

The Battle of Naseby

On 14 June 1645 the otherwise unremarkable tenor of life in the parish of Naseby was briefly disturbed by a battle on its soil which made its name more famous than that of almost any other village in the country. This was the decisive engagement of the Civil War fought between King Charles I and Parliament.

Before Naseby the scales had been fairly evenly balanced, but in 1644 parliament reformed its army as the New Model, strengthened by the calling in of scattered garrisons. Sir Thomas Fairfax was appointed Commander-in-Chief, with Oliver Cromwell as Lieutenant-General of the Horse and Major-General Skippon to command the Foot. Fairfax was able at last to give his army its proper task of bringing the King's main field army to battle, and he moved accordingly.

In response to this threat the King assembled his army in the Midlands and sent urgent orders to Lord Goring, commanding the army of the West, to join him. The King moved irresolutely about the south midlands, but Goring never came. His disobedience spelled the ruin of the royal cause at Naseby.

June 11 found the King at Fawsley near Daventry while Fairfax and the new Model had advanced *via* Wootton, Northampton and Kislingbury, and there was a skirmish only two miles from Daventry. The royal army stood to arms on Borough Hill that night but slipped away next morning towards Market Harborough, hoping still to avoid combat until reinforcements arrived. Fairfax followed and on June 13 Ireton, with the strong party of parliamentary horse overran a royalist rear-guard in Naseby, the King having reached Market Harborough.

At sunrise on the 14th his army marched up to the ridge between Farndon and Oxendon and were drawn up in order of battle facing southwards towards Naseby. It was a fine morning and the Roundhead army was clearly visible on the Naseby ridge eight miles away at a point near where the Fitzgerald obelisk was later erected. Cromwell advised Fairfax that the position was unsuitable for battle as Prince Rupert would never attack up such a steep slope, nor would his horse pass over the marshy ground at the foot. Accordingly, Fairfax ordered a move westwards towards Mill Hill. Prince Rupert rode out with his lifeguard to reconnoitre and sent urgent orders to the army to follow. This they did as far as Dust

Hill, where, looking southwards across a shallow valley they saw the Roundhead army drawn up facing them on Redhill ridge and all was set for battle.

On the parliamentary right wing Cromwell commanded 3,250 Horse, with Colonel Whalley as second in command. In the centre Skippon commanded 6,400 Foot, Pikemen and Musketeers. Ireton, commanding another 2,700 Horse, had the left wing, and beyond, and at right angles, there was a force of 800 dragoons (mounted infantry) under Colonel Okey lining Sulby boundary hedge. In front of the centre was a skirmishing party of musketeers called in those days "the forlorn hope". Behind the centre, Fairfax had a strong reserve of Foot.

The Royalists adopted the same formation of Horse on the wings and Foot in the centre. On the right wing Prince Rupert and Prince Maurice commanded the flower of the royal cavalry. Lord Astley commanded the Foot in the centre and Langdale had the Northern Horse and the Newark Horse on the left. The King himself, with his Lifeguards, formed a reserve behind the centre, including two *corps d'elite* of Foot, the King's Own Regiment, and Rupert's Bluecoats. This was the order of battle at ten in the morning when the royal army, 7,500 strong, advanced to the attack against 14,000.

The quality of the royal Foot and the Prince's cavalry was very high. They were veteran troops, ably led. Langdale's Horse were of less certain quality and the absence of Goring's splendid cavalry told severely. Those present advanced loyally down the slope from Dust Hill on to Broadmoor, the line gay with colours and described by eye witnesses as 'in the most gallant array'.

Walking their horses the wings kept line with the Foot in the centre as they approached the Roundhead line. Then the Prince's Horse smashed into Ireton at a gallop and after a stiff fight at sword point, broke the Roundhead wing, and drove them off the field. English Cavalry has always been difficult to halt and reform after a successful charge, and the cavaliers at Naseby were no exception. They lacked stern discipline and would not be halted in the chase after their flying enemy. Only the resistance of the musketeers guarding the Roundhead baggage train checked them far behind the battle. Eventually they re-formed and rode slowly back with blown horses and exhausted men too late to affect the course of the battle.

Astley's Foot in the centre fired one valley and then waded in with clubbed muskets and 'push of pike'. The whole Roundhead centre broke in confusion, many leaving their colours in disorder to fall behind the reserves. Both sides now reinforced their centre, Fairfax leading his reserve forward and the King launched his two reserve regiments. Deadlock resulted. All now depended on the cavalry of the Roundhead right under Cromwell. He did not wait to be attacked but sent his leading regiments down the slope against the Northern Horse, retaining his second line under his own hand. Whalley broke the Northern Horse and drove them off the field whereupon Cromwell wheeled his second line and launched them at the left flank of the royal infantry. Okey remounted his Dragoons at Sulby Hedge and brought them in line against Astley's right flank.

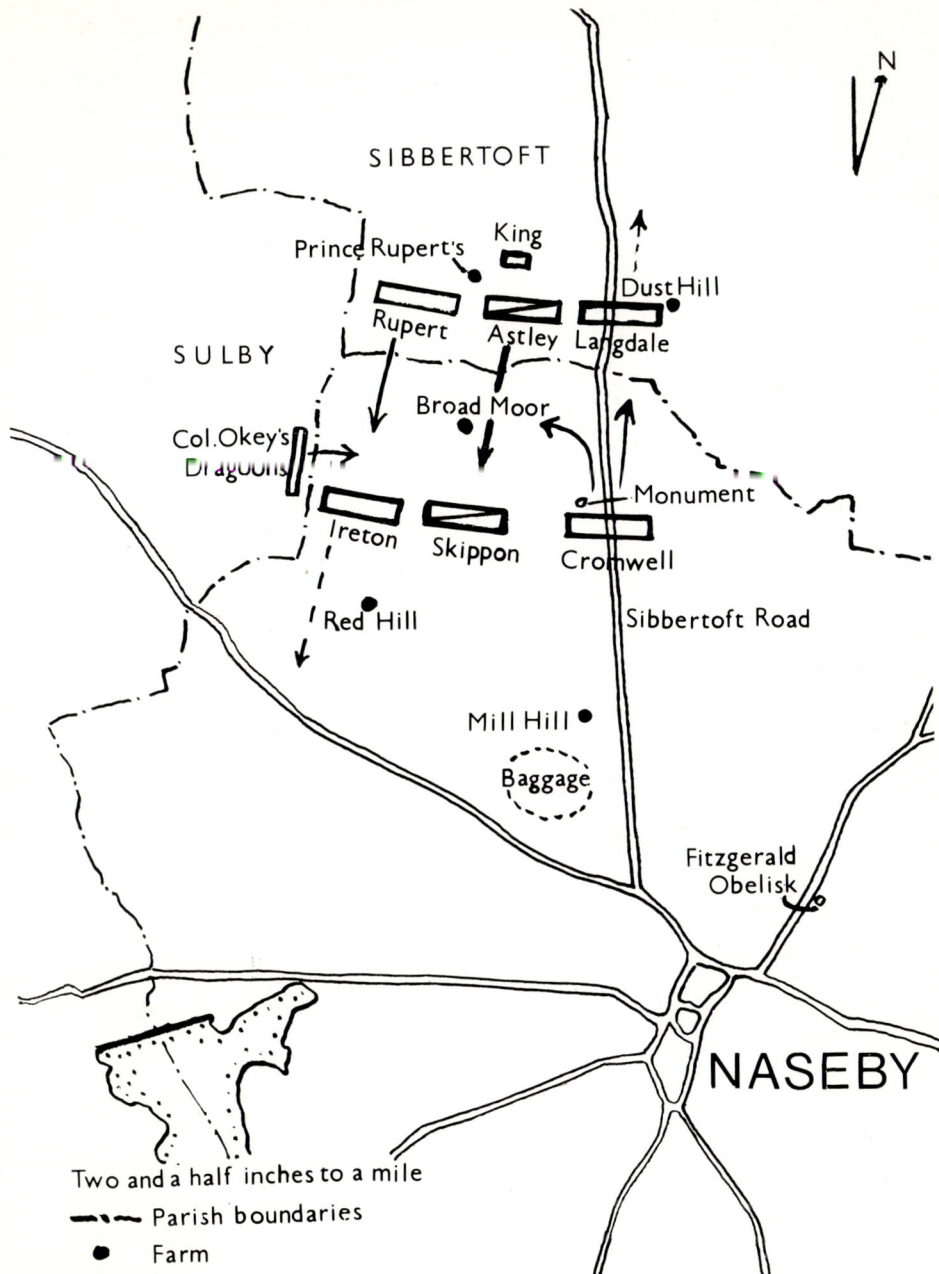

SIBBERTOFT

Prince Rupert's   King   Dust Hill

Rupert   Astley   Langdale

SULBY

Broad Moor

Col. Okey's
Dragoons

Monument

Ireton   Skippon   Cromwell

Red Hill   Sibbertoft Road

Mill Hill

Baggage

Fitzgerald
Obelisk

NASEBY

Two and a half inches to a mile

Parish boundaries

Farm

THE BATTLE OF NASEBY 1645

15

The royal Foot was now surrounded and retreated down the slope on to Broadmoor. Here most of them surrendered, but Rupert's Bluecoats fought on until they were killed as they stood in a square, almost to a man. The only intact force now left to the King was his small reserve of Horse on Dust Hill. These he attempted to lead forward to the help of his stricken Foot but the attempt was frustrated. Someone seized the King's bridle and turned his horse, while someone else gave the order 'March to the Right'.

The whole reserve rode off the field carrying the King with them, pursued by Roundhead cavalry as far as Leicester and beyond. Superior numbers and superior discipline had won the day. The King's field army was broken beyond repair and the parliamentary cause had triumphed.

This great battle was not recorded in the parish register, nor, it seems, in any other local document. It occupied, or so it seems, only a small place in the folk memories of the village. Mastin observed in 1792 that an old villager remembered a Naseby man who had been present at the burial of the dead in a communal grave on the battlefield, the country people 'coming in from all quarters' to help. Occasionally shot and iron fragments were turned up by the plough in subsequent periods. The table around which the King's rear guard had been drinking when surprised by Ireton stayed in the village with other battle relics in the possession of the Ashby family and is now in the parish church. And there was a legend that the body of Cromwell was secretly buried in Naseby after the desecration of his tomb after the Restoration. But the battle faded in importance in the Naseby consciousness until its memory was revived for propaganda as well as antiquarian purposes in Victorian times.

Later Stuart and Georgian Naseby

From an analysis of the totals of baptisms and burials each decade listed in the parish registers (see graph on page 17) it would seem that there was a rise in the population in the Elizabethan period. In the next period the fifty years after 1603, the increase of baptisms over burials was smaller indicating a slackening of the increase in population, and in the decade 1633-43 there was for the first and only time in the parish registers an overplus of deaths over baptisms. We know that there were disastrous visitations of the plague to Northamptonshire in this half century, the worst being that of 1638: it looks very much as though Naseby fell victim to it. A comparison of the surnames of Naseby villagers given on the map of 1630 with those on the hearth tax list of 1662 shows a startling fact which perhaps bears this out. In 1662 only nine householders had surnames which appear on the 1630 map. Even allowing for the imperfection of these sources this seems to have been a remarkable changeover in the people of the village. Perhaps this may have been caused by the war, but it would seem more likely to have been caused by an epidemic, new families taking over the houses and land of the plague victims. After 1653 the gap between baptisms and burials widens dramatically and it would seem that once more the population was increasing markedly.

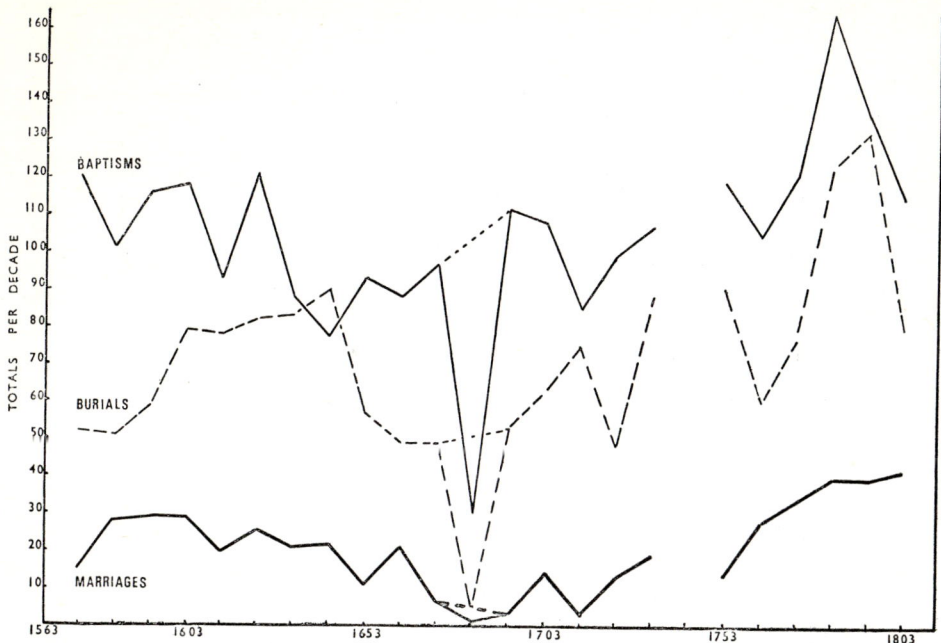

GRAPH OF MARRIAGES, BAPTISMS AND BURIALS IN NASEBY 1563-1803

Totals decade by decade calculated from the parish registers. Dotted lines in the 1680s and gaps in the mid 18th century indicate incomplete or missing data.

It is not until the year 1676 that we can find reasonably reliable information on the size of Naseby's population. In that year the 'Compton Return' reports that the population consisted of '70 families', comprising '400 persons young and old', '0 Popish recusants' and '1 Obstinate Separatist'.[13] This figure for the number of families or households accords reasonably well with the assessment for the Hearth Tax taken in 1674 which revealed that the 74 houses had 95 hearths in them.[14] In 1720 John Bridges estimated the number of families at 'about 90' showing that the population had increased in the previous forty years or so. But by the end of the eighteenth century the population had not increased very much more, Mastin estimating that there were 100 houses and about 600 people there in 1792. He probably *over*-estimated, because the first census (1801) arrived at a figure of only 538, though there might well have been migration from Naseby in the hard years of the 1790s.

Not a lot is known about Naseby in the 18th century. The probate inventory of Samuel Harbert (or Herbert) who died in 1723 gives detailed information about the possessions and stock of one large farmer. He farmed 'seven and a half yard lands in Naseby field' (probably between 220 and 300 acres); had a flock of over 200 sheep, including 13 at Guilsborough, 51 at Kelmarsh and a 'one third share of 19 other sheep

17

in Naseby field', and his 59 cattle included ten cows and a 'bull stag' at Kelmarsh, and a half share in ten Welsh heifers at Naseby. The Herberts were still prominent farmers half a century later, and there were one or two other large farmers, notably the Everards who lived at Shuckburgh house. However, the traditional pattern of small farms remained largely unchanged in 18th century Naseby.

The militia list of 1777, which gives the names and occupations of the sixty-four men between the ages of 18 and 45 in the parish liable for service gives some idea of the economic structure of the village in the early reign of George III. Twenty-one of the men were farmers and a further 26 were servants, labourers and shepherds. Of the rest, seven were worsted weavers, two shoemakers, two tailors, there was a carpenter, a joiner, a blacksmith, a horse-collar maker, leaving two who were infirm.[15] It was a small farming community, worsted weaving alone offering much of an alternative as an occupation to the villagers if they stayed in Naseby.

During the 18th century the larger of the two Naseby estates changed hands. What had happened to it between 1522 and 1720 is not clear. There can be no doubt that it was soon resold by Sir William Fitzwilliam to whom it was granted in 1522 for it was never part of the Fitzwilliam of Milton estates. At the beginning of the 18th century it was in the possession of a Sir John Wolstenholm who conveyed it to Charles Joye in 1720, the year of the South Sea Bubble, Bridges noting that the purchase money was £14,500. It was Joye who pulled down and rebuilt the Manor House (now Manor Farm). Seventy years later in 1792 the owner of the estate was a Leicestershire gentleman, Sir Isaac Pocock, who had acquired it on marriage to the relict of a Peter Joye, esquire, of Benefield.

The other estate, the inheritance of the Shuckburghs, remained in the hands of their Ashby decendants right through the century, passing from George Ashby to his son Waring Ashby and then to his grandson, another George, who was in possession in 1792.

Part III   Naseby since 1792

On the eve of enclosure

The parliamentary act for the enclosure of Naseby was passed in 1820, and by early 1823 the open-field system had vanished for ever. A detailed account of the village and parish on the eve of this process appears in *The History and Antiquities of Naseby in the County of Northampton* by the Reverend John Mastin, the first edition of which was published by subscription in 1792, a second appearing in 1818. Mastin had been curate of Naseby from 1778 and in 1783 succeeded to the living. He was incumbent until his death in the year 1829 at the ripe old age of 81.

Just under half of his *History* is devoted to an account of the battle of Naseby, and there seems little doubt that the author's main intention in producing the work was to put his rather remote parish on the map as a place to which antiquarians could make an excursion at once scholarly and pleasurable. But interesting though Mastin's account of the battle is, it is his description of Naseby itself about the year 1792 that makes the book valuable to local historians. In his account of Naseby's situation, of the pleasures of the open air life and of rural sports, Mastin catches the spirit of the Northamptonshire countryside in the eighteenth century. Set on its hill in the rolling Midland landscape he declared Naseby to be 'a delightful summer residence, presenting to the eye almost unbounded prospects. A finer landscape can scarcely be painted by art, than is here represented by nature's pencil. It is no exaggeration to say, that thirty nine, or forty parish churches may be seen from one station, and old windmill bank in Naseby field'. The only objection which could be made to such a residence were the badness of the roads in winter 'and a deep heavy country', but the roads were in an improving state, and a few more years would be tolerably good, he thought.

Naseby, he observed, was a fine place for sportsmen. 'If one be fond of hunting, Naseby is by no means an inconvenient situation, being within reach of the foxhounds of Althorpe and Pitchley'; if fond of coursing, one 'cannot wish for a finer field, not a hedge, or a tree for more than a mile together, a few scattered thorns only and patches of gorse or furze. Here at some seasons is a plenty of hares; and sportsmen often come to try their dogs in Naseby field'. In the shooting season partridges were plentiful, and some winters snipe were in abundance. Mastin, like that other eighteenth century antiquarian parson the Reverend John Morton, author of *The Natural History of Northamptonshire,* 1712, delighted in describing the soils, springs, fossils, and flora and fauna. 'Here are wild geese and ducks, and plenty of grey and often whistling plover . . . [and] the large white-headed eagle, said to be a native of Norway, Denmark and Lapland, has been seen for two-winters, for a short-time.'

Mastin paints a graphic picture of the village at this time. Apart from the church, the manor house, the vicarage (which had been rebuilt for him in 1785 by his patron Mr. Ashby — to whom he dedicated his book), and Shuckburgh house, it was almost entirely cob cottages covered with thatch. The material from which these cottages were constructed was 'a kind of kealy earth . . . excellent of its kind, and the best calculated for building I ever saw; walls built with this earth are exceedingly firm and strong, and if kept dry, are said to be more durable than if built with soft stone or indifferent bricks'. It is true, Mastin admitted, that the external appearance of these cottages could have been improved, but, alas, the only 'new coat which they have once a year consists of cow dung spread upon them to dry for firing, but as the present occupiers are only tenants at will,

---

(Overleaf) VIEW FROM BACK STREET (NOW HIGH STREET) NASEBY IN 1855
Photograph by the Rev. W. Law showing the almost African appearance of Naseby with its cob cottages and cob walls. Sold to raise money for church restoration, it shows the stump and ball of the Church before the spire was completed.

Naseby
Sep.t 25.th 1855
WL

improvements . . . are hardly to be expected'. Many of the oldest houses were of cruck construction which Mastin described as 'forked building, which forks are all of oak, very rough, strong, uncouth, and put together in a rude manner'. The cob cottages of Naseby remained until an improving landlord in the 1870s and the local authority housing committee in the inter-war period replaced them, giving the village housing its modern spick-and-span appearance.

Mastin supplies detailed information on the open field topography and the economy of Naseby in the generation before enclosure. His account is critical and is basically in accord with William Pitt's observations on the parish in his *General View of the Agriculture of the County of North-hampton* (1813). Pitt saw the open field, 'extensive and in as backward a state as it could be in Charles the First's time, when the fatal battle was fought. The lower parts a moist range pasture, with furze, rushes, and ferns abounding; the rest of the field a strong, brown, deep loam, in the usual bean and wheat culture. Pasture enclosures near the village, and a good many cows kept. *The parish is as much in a state of nature as anything I have seen in the county*. The avenues across the field to the village zig-zag, as chance had directed, with the hollows and sloughs emptied, except with mire'.

Mastin was an ardent improver and encloser and was as dissatisfied by what he saw of the farming of the parish as Pitt was to be. He declared that 'no field in Northamptonshire would answer better by inclosure than that of Naseby. Here is good strong land, fine slades for meadows; red hills, good for turnips and artificial grasses, black woodcock, or falling ground, now grass, but much to be improved by plowing. Some few bogs, which might either by under-draining be laid dry, or rendered still more valuable by being planted'.[16] The farming community consisted of twenty-one farmers 'who keep teams' and they in turn supported four blacksmiths, two wheelwrights, a horse collar-maker and saddler, several carpenters, six shoemakers, two butchers, a baker, and an army of labourers. He describes the immutable and essentially primitive three field rotation; 'the mode of husbandry is regular, as to the culture; the lordship being divided into three parts, not by fences, but by marks made in the ground, called field-marks, so that there may be said to be three fields; viz. one, wheat, rye and barley; one, beans and oats; and one fallow. Every field has certain portion of red, or kealy soil, upon which is sown rye, the stronger and blacker lands are sown with wheat and barley, and this always after a fallow. Oats are sown after rye, and beans after wheat and barley'.[17]

Naseby was no place for go-ahead improvers. Traditional farming practice was so strong that, in Mastin's opinion, 'a man ever so ingenious in agriculture, hath no opportunity of displaying his abilities at Naseby. He is confined to old customs, and can only do the same thing with his neighbours. The tenants are certainly blind to their own interest, having every year an opportunity of sowing their red land with turnips, which they totally neglect; they cannot be ignorant of the advantage of this mode of husbandry, as it is often practised in open fields, and, I believe, generally at Rothwell in this neighbourhood'.[18]

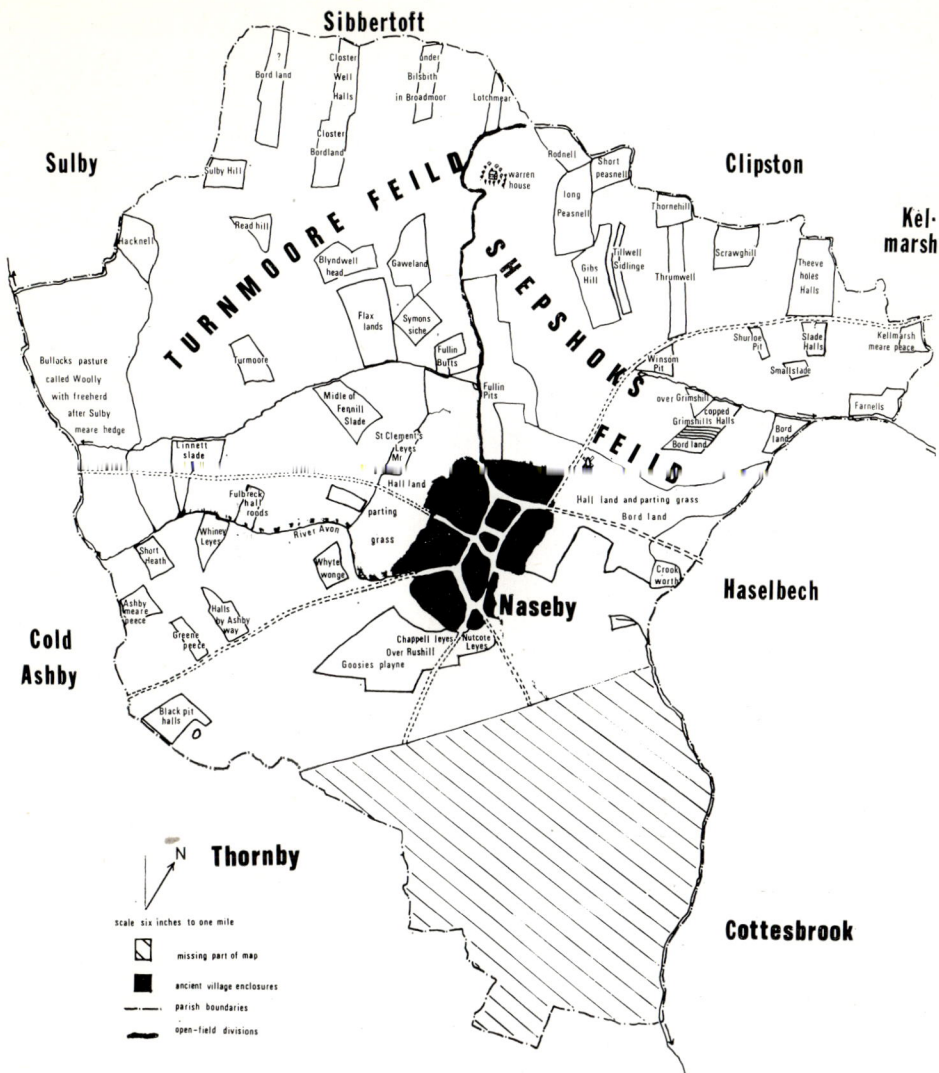

Map labels:

Sibbertoft

Sulby

Clipston

Kel-marsh

Closter Well Halls
Bord land
under Bilsoth in Broadmoor
Lotchmear
Closter Bordland
Sulby Hill
Head hill
Hacknell

TURNMOORE FEILD

Blyndwell head
Gaweland
Flax lands
Symons siche
Fullin Butts
Fullin Pitts

SHEPSHOKS FEILD

Rodnell
Short peasnell
long Peasnell
warren house
Gibs Hill
Tullwell Sidlinge
Thrumwell
Thornehill
Scrawghill
Theeve holes Halls

Bullocks pasture
called Woolly
with freeherd
after Sulby
meare hedge
Turmoore
Midle of Fennill Slade
St Clement's Leyes Mr
Linnett slade
Hall land
Fulbreck half roods
parting
grass
Whiney Leyes
River Avon
Short Heath
Whyte wonges
Ashby meare peece
Halls by Ashby way
Greene peece
Black pit halls

Wensom Pit
over Grimshill
Grimshills Halls
copped
Bord land
Shurlock Pit
Slade Halls
Smallslade
Kellmarsh meare peace
Farnells
Bord land

Hall land and parting grass
Bord land
Crook worth

Naseby

Haselbech

Cold Ashby

Chappell leyes
Over Rushill
Goosies playne
Nutcote Leyes

N
Thornby

scale six inches to one mile

☒ missing part of map
■ ancient village enclosures
—·—·— parish boundaries
▬▬▬ open-field divisions

Cottesbrook

ESTATE MAP OF THE LORD OF THE MANOR AND CHIEF LANDOWNER IN 1630
It shows the way holdings were scattered in the open fields. Unfortunately there is no indication as to the landowner for whom the map was made. *Meare* is the old name for boundary, *bord land* was land held by bordage tenure, i.e. by men of bordar status. NOTE the warren house in Shepshoks field.

Naseby was enclosed late, and this failure may well have caused the enterprising to move out of the village. In a footnote in the second edition of his history Mastin observed, 'Families of the name of King and Watts have emigrated to Northumberland, Pennsylvania, the former a mechanic

23

. . . the latter purchased a farm . . . which he has cultivated with encouraging success'.

He gives precise figures of the stock on Naseby farms in 1792 — 2,800 sheep, 360 cows and about 300 mares. There was nothing remarkable in the breeds, he declared, though he does say that Arthur Young had commented favourably on the pigs some years before. The cows had improved recently, he observed, because Mr. Ashby had presented his tenants with good bulls. 'The cows lie in the farm yards during winter, and upon the 12th of May go to pasturage in the field, in two herds, called the upper and lower herd, where they have liberty to graze till St. Andrew, old stile [30 November]. They are kept by men, who have one shilling and six-pence per head for their work.'[19]

The sheep, though kept in as large numbers as formerly, were not as profitable as might be expected, 'numbers of them dying in the winter season for want of shelter and pasturage, and sometimes they are subject to a spring or summer rot. This chiefly arises from the neglect of draining, which is the more to be lamented, because the ground, if laid dry, would become sound land . . . . They *practise* a mode of draining with a large plow, called the town plow, made exceedingly strong in every part, having two coulters: it cuts a drain one foot deep and wide, and throws out the earth the same distance from the side on the right hand. This plow is drawn by ten or twelve horses, a team made by as many farmers contributing each his horse. But this scheme, from the obstinacy and perverseness of some, is often rendered abortive. They put back into the drain the earth thrown out, to prevent, as they say, its lying in the way of the scythe at hay time'.[20]

He noted that the tenants stocked by the yard—land 'which consists of no determinate number of acres, but is the same as oxgangs, or oxhuts, as they are called in the vale of Belvoir, and many other parts of England; and in old law books, signifies in some counties fifteen acres, and in others twenty; in some twenty four, and in others thirty of forty acres: these differ exceedingly with respect to the quality of arable; but all of them carry the same stock', and refers to an old agreement as to the method of grazing the cattle: 'Some years ago, likewise, the cows, in the summer months, were kept by the respective occupiers, upon grass land dispersed about the field, every man keeping his beasts upon his own land. But this mode being found not only vexatious, but ruinous, it was agreed in 1733 that pastures should be taken from the extremities of the field, to which every man should contribute grass land in proportion to his flock; this, by reference, was settled, and the land appropriated for this purpose, entered into a book as a proper terrier, to prevent confusion at any future time, and the cows now, as I before observed, go in herds'.[21]

One feature of open-field Naseby was that at the time of the enclosure act there were, apparently, no commons or waste. In the words of Mastin, 'It is remarkable that the whole should be known land: a singular circumstance in open fields when there is so much pasture'.

Naseby had perhaps never been a rich place, but Mastin observed that there was an increase in poverty in the village at the time he was writing.

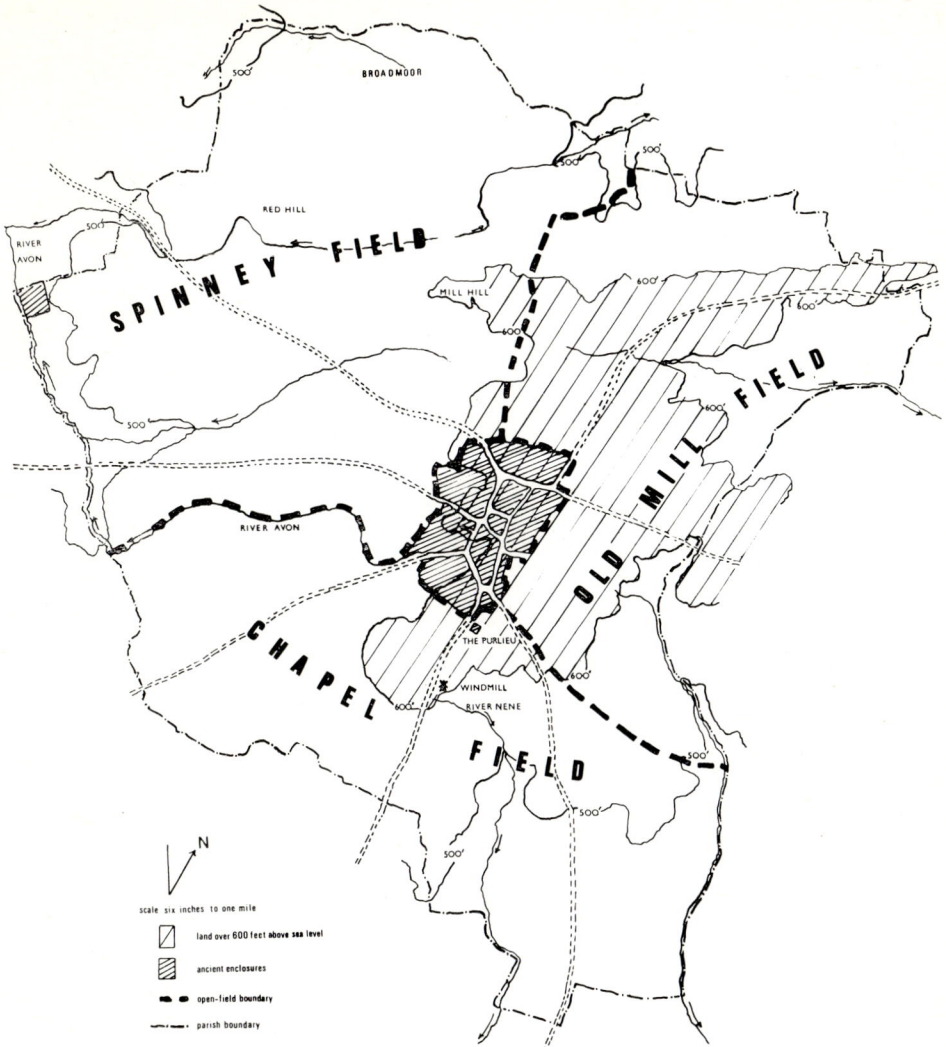

NASEBY BEFORE ENCLOSURE

Unfortunately no map of the furlongs, slades, commons, etc. of the open field system survives. However, a comparison of the features on this map with the estate map of 1630 gives some idea of old Naseby field and of the topographical logic of the open field system. NOTE how the field names have changed.

He connected this with the decline of the principal non-agricultural pursuit in the village. The only industry of note 'carried on here is weaving harateens, and tammys, and the spinning jersey by the women, at the long wheel, for the master weavers. Many families are employed in this work, and, when trade is good, earn a tolerable competency; when bad, as it has long been, a great deal of work is expected to be done for little money, and the most industrious poor have been almost starved. In consequence the poor rates have advanced very considerably within the last twenty or thirty years; from fifty to two hundred pounds per annum: the late return to parliament was that sum'.[22] The returns to Parliament by overseas of the poor for 1777, 1787, 1803 and 1813, show Mastin to have been only too correct. In 1776-7 Naseby spent £126 on its poor, in 1783-5 about the same on average each of the three years, but there was a sharp rise in the nineties, £340 being the amount spent in 1802-3. This was to rise sharply again in the next decade, reaching a peak of £716 in the year 1812-13.

On this growth in poverty Mastin makes the shrewd comment that 'Inclosures have been condemned for having this bad effect, but the above is demonstrative proof they are not always the cause; they have risen here as rapidly in proportion as in inclosed lordships, and are sure to be found high in every place where manufactories are carried on'.[23] Under-estimating the extent to which the population of the village, and indeed the country as a whole, was rising in this period, and also the completeness of the collapse of the Northamptonshire worsted-weaving and wool-combing industry in the early 1790s, Mastin attributed this increase mainly to improvidence and indiscipline — 'the mechanics are too much their own masters and few of them are disposed to work the whole of their time. Monday and sometimes Tuesday, is appropriated to pleasure, if not to scenes of riot and intemperance . . . . They fulfil the scripture phrase (but in a sense never meant) that "take no thought for the morrow", at least it is so in too many places. Consequently when calamities of any sort overtake them, being destitute of the means of helping themselves, they apply to the parish for relief'.[24]

He was careful to say that this was not the case with *all* of the poor, for many were members of the village Friendly Society, 'a most benevolent institution, called the Amicable Society, consisting of inferior tradesmen and cottagers, has of late years been established in this parish; by a weekly deposit, made of each member, a fund is raised to support such of their brethren and families, as by sickness, or other misfortunes may be rendered incapable of providing for themselves. The management of the whole is by two stewards, chosen annually, by the majority of their own members, the number of which, this year, is forty-two: the good effects of this establishment are visible to all. The audit . . . is, at the particular desire of a great promoter of this charity, annually to be held on Christmas day, and after attending the duties of the church, and hearing a sermon preached upon the occasion'.[25]

Mastin's book tells us a little about village customs. The wake was kept on the Sunday after All Saints (the Sunday following 1 November) each year; and the great holiday of the year, the 'feast', celebrated all over Northamptonshire, was on Trinity Monday (one week after Whit Monday) at Naseby, the 'inhabitants inviting their friends, and making merry; the young people assemble, and spend the afternoon and evening with ringing of bells, dancing, etc. It is called here, Rothwell Fair Monday; this custom probably arose from a large fair at that place, the eight or nine miles distant'.

On village government Mastin noted one apparently odd omission. 'A manor court has not been held for many years, because, as I have been informed, there are no tenants to it.' It is not clear what Mastin meant by this, and it is unclear how the farmers settled disputes arising out of working the open fields, without such a Court. However, the practice of holding manorial courts evidently revived, for records survive for the years 1803, 1804-6, 1808, 1814, 1817, 1820, 1823 and 1825. Those up to 1820 contain details of the usual appointments of constables, fieldkeepers, pindars, and so on, and the regulations agreed to for keeping roads clear, preventing encroachments, scouring water courses, stinting (apportioning) and stocking commons and the multi-farious other issues which had to be agreed on co-operatively to work the old open-field system.

The enclosure of Naseby 1020-1022

An important question which arises about the enclosure of the parish is why was it that Naseby was enclosed so much later than most of the neighbouring parishes? We can only speculate, but it seems likely that the Pococks, the largest of the two landowners, who were also rather remote from the place, were unwilling to bear the heavy cost and had opposed it. However, between 1817 and 1820 the Pocock estate, comprising some two thirds of the parish of Naseby, passed to John Purcell Fitzgerald, a Lancashire landowner and coal-mine proprietor. He had been born John Purcell and had adopted the surname of his wife, an heiress who brought him extensive lands in other counties, and through her inheritance he became chief proprietor and lord of the manor of Naseby.

The Fitzgeralds, in the early years at any rate, seem willing to have been active leaders in Naseby. An enclosure act was promptly got through parliament, they renovated the parish church, gave a piece of land to the Methodists for a much-desired chapel in the village, caused the stump of the old market cross to be removed from its corner of the churchyard, and erected a large one of celtic style in its place. It was never inscribed and it stands to this day an oddly purposeless memorial. (The shaft of the ancient market cross was re-erected on the edge of the village, in front of the present village hall). And the Fitzgeralds (who evidently loved monuments) erected in 1823 a large inscribed obelisk to commemorate the battle of Naseby. It also seems that they built the Hall at Naseby Woolleys, the only considerable mansion in the parish, about which the Reverend Henry Lockinge in his *Historical Gleanings on the Memorable Field of Naseby* (1830) commented that the visitor 'Amid the peaceful charm of its groves and shrubberies — will not easily persuade himself — that it was but a very few years before a sterile morass'.

The Naseby Inclosure Act was passed on 8 July 1820. Its purposes were stated as 'the dividing allotting and Inclosing and otherwise improving all the Open and Common Fields Wastes and Other Commonable Lands in the Parish of Naseby and for exonerating from Tythes all the Lands in the said Parish as well open as inclosed'. Commissioners and surveyors were appointed, and proceeded to carry out the requirements of this Act, making their award on 20 December 1822.

The three parts into which Naseby field had been divided in 1820 — Spinney Field, Old Mill Field, and Chapel Field — disappeared, and the proprietors of the land had their holdings re-awarded to them in convenient blocks. John Fitzgerald, in right of Frances his wife, received almost exactly two thirds of the parish (2,078 acres) and John Maddock, in right of his wife Hannah Maria, Heiress of the Shuckburgh/Ashby inheritance, received almost all the rest (1,060 acres). The Grand Union Canal Company were awarded 62 acres for access to the reservoir in the parish, the church-wardens of Naseby received 12 acres, and the four public gravel pits and the public sheepwash totalled four acres.

As the map on page 29 shows, Fitzgerald land was in a discrete block from a line drawn north north west from the village round clockwise to a line drawn south south west, with a detached estate of about 250 acres in the west corner of the parish. Quite why this piece was separate is not clear, but on it Naseby Woolleys Hall with its 80 acres of shrubs, lakes and gardens was laid out, presumably for the enjoyment of the Fitzgeralds. It has remained a hunting lodge, or shooting box, ever since. In 1858-9 249 acres of the Naseby Woolleys estate was exchanged by Viscount Clifden (who had by then bought the Fitzgerald estate) with Captain George Ashby Ashby the heir to the Ashby/Maddock estate, and the captain moved into Naseby Woolleys Hall, thus completing the consolidation of the estates which the enclosure Commissioners started.[26]

Following the enclosure two brickyards (one for each estate?) were opened in Naseby, and a start was made in building ring-fence farms away from the village. Dates on their bricks show that New Hall farm, Woolleys farm and the Grange were all built in 1822, and the cottage at Mill Hill farm has bricks dated 1830. But this process had not gone far by the time of the 1851 census. The enumerators' schedules show that all but seven of the farmers still had addresses in the village itself. It is possible that the Fitzgeralds at any rate had run into financial trouble by then and had been unable to carry on farm building. They sold the estate in 1855, and we know that to pay for his share of the costs of the enclosure John Fitzgerald had to take out a mortgage for £10,390, the land costing £5 an acre to enclose.[27]

In addition to straightening the winding roads of the parish, the com-missioners also laid out several new ones which went straight as dies across the landscape, the roads to Sibbertoft, due north out of the village, and 'Coal Pit lane' (now Carvell's lane) due west, being the most striking examples. To metal these roads they opened four 'stone, chalk rubble, and gravel pits'. The commissioners also ordered three 'drains' to be made. This involved digging out and straightening the streams which ran westward from the village, and just north of it, respectively, into the canal reservoir and the river Avon.

The commissioners also supervised the exchange of ownership of houses, cottages, gardens in the village which had been anciently enclosed. (The

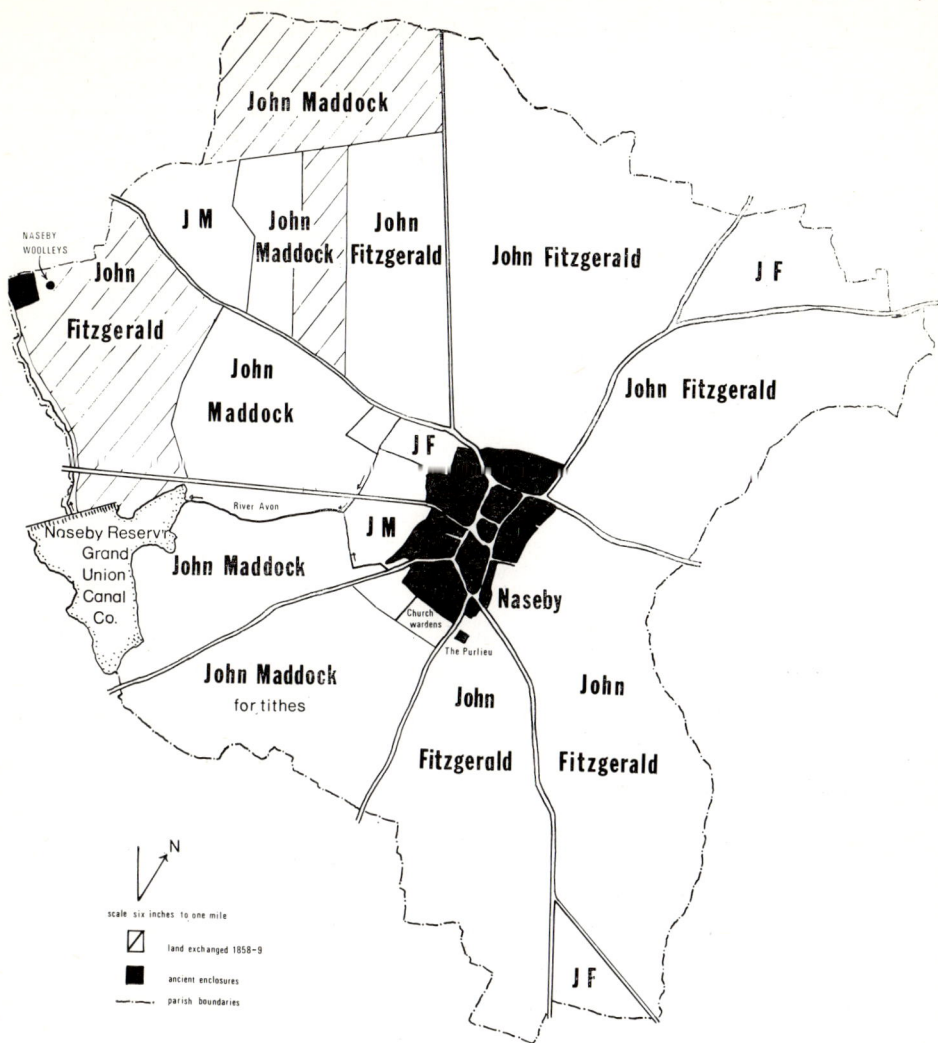

THE ENCLOSURE OF NASEBY 1820-22

only enclosed parts of the parish *outside* the village were 'the purlieu' just
south of it, and a small portion right on the parish boundary on the north
west). Apart from the vicar's tiny freehold of 2 rods 5 perches, the church
and churchyard itself, and the churchwardens' 12 acres, all the ancient village
enclosures were owned by Fitzgerald and Maddock. Fitzgerald came out
with 81 acres of tenements and orchards (mostly on the east or High Street
side of the village) and Maddock with 30 acres on the west or Church
Street side.

The last manorial courts for which we have records — those held in 1823 and 1825 — give brief glimpses of the end of the old organisation of farming. The offices of thirdbearers and field keepers were not filled because these had become obsolete now the open fields had gone. In 1823 is was presented that the lanes had been stocked with cows, sheep and asses by persons with no right there, and it was ordered that until some further court order be made no stock of any kind was to be allowed on the roads. The pinder was ordered to impound any animal found there, a penalty of 2/6d. to be paid by their owners for every pig or sheep, over and above the pinder's customary fees. At this court it was also agreed that no servant should be hired so as to gain a settlement in Naseby by any bargain to be made after this time. The rate-payers were worried about rising poor rates, but it may also be that the completion of the enclosure hedging, fence-building and ditch digging was achieved and there were fewer jobs about.

On 15 April 1825 we have the last record of a Manorial Court. There was no business transacted.[28]

The Population of Victorian Naseby

An outline of the economic fortunes of Naseby from 1801 can be deduced from the population figures revealed by the decennial censuses, shown in figure 1.

Figure 1. The Population of Naseby 1801-1951

Year	Census Population
1801	538
1811	598
1821	697
1831	707
1841	898*
1851	849
1861	812
1871	693
1881	610
1891	551
1901	476
1911	456
1921	416
1931	399
1951	346

* includes '48 persons attending the annual feast'

Contrary to popular legend, enclosures did not generally lead to a rapid migration off the land. Certainly this was the case in Naseby. The population increased substantially in the ten years before the enclosure, remained steady in the decade following, and then increased more rapidly than ever before in the 1830s. The 1840s saw the village population at its peak, and it was only in the last forty years of the century that the migration of the labourers took place, spurred by the agricultural depression of the seventies and eighties.

There had of course been a steady migration of talent away from Naseby from the early part of the century. The *Northampton Daily Chronicle* 20 March 1914, for instance, tells us of the success story of John Haddon, the son of a farmer whose family had farmed there since 1590. As a boy he had been apprenticed to a printer in Clipston who, on removal to Dunstable, took his apprentice with him. In 1814, at the age of twenty, he went to London and started the firm which became John Haddon and Co., printers, engineers and furnishers, at the Caxton Type-Foundry and Wood Mills, London. In 1914 the firm, then being run by the third generation of Haddons, issued a centenary souvenir history. Another success story was that of John Hampson a Naseby man who became editor of the *Bedfordshire Times*.[29] Again, in April 1914 the Vestry Minute books record that the vicar had received a gift of £5 from the Hon. S. S. Burdett of Washington, U.S.A., whose father, Cheney Burdett, had been baptised at Naseby in 1785 and had presumably emigrated, like many others, in the bad years of the early 19th century.

An analysis of the 1851 and 1871 Census Enumerators' schedules gives a detailed picture of the people of mid-Victorian Naseby.[30] In 1851 the population of 849 people were made up of 177 households living in 173 houses. The most obvious feature (and it was a characteristic of the nation as a whole at this time) was the youthfulness of the population. Forty three per cent of the people were children of 14 years and under, just over half (53%) were aged 19 years or less, and a further 13% were in their twenties. In other words, two thirds of the people of Naseby in 1851 had been born since 1821. The rest of the population was made up of those in the age groups 30-59 years (27%) whilst those of 60 years and over amounted to only 7 per cent of the total. The great majority of these people were Naseby born or came from villages within a five-mile radius.

The social structure of Naseby in 1851 was uncomplicated. It consisted of farmers, craftsmen and shopkeepers, and a large class of labourers, lace-workers and servants. The middle-class was represented by the tenant of Naseby Hall, a Mr. George A. Crump who hailed from Liverpool, and had possibly been an East India merchant, for his wife had been born in Calcutta. Crump was a recent arrival (certainly since 1849 for he is not mentioned in Whellan's directory for that year) and is possibly the first of a long line of well-to-do outsiders to rent or purchase the desirable country residence of Naseby Woolleys. The only other member of the middle-class was the vicar, the Rev. James Jones, a Welshman.

There were twenty two farmers in Naseby in 1851 (compared to the twenty-one mentioned by Mastin in 1792) and information about them from the census schedule is summarised in figure 2.

Figure 2.   Farmers in 1851

Farmer	Address	Acreage	No. of Employees
Joseph Bassett	Bassett Lodge	505	10
John Smeeton	Woolleys Lodge	290	9
Joseph Smeeton	Broadmoor Lodge	230	6
Sarah Everard	Front St.	210	4
Thomas Watts	Front St.	200	5
James Clay	Front St.	191	4
John Everard	Naseby Lodge	191	4
Samuel Wright	Naseby Lodge	179	6
Charles Watcham	Front St.	158	5
John B. Smeeton	Front St.	150	4
David Everard	Back St.	150	2
William Hadden	Back St.	120	4
John Everard	Back Street	104	2
Nathaniel Frisby	Back St.	103	3
Richard Hadden	Back St.	100	3
John Ilston	Front St.	100	4
William Henson	Henson Lodge	86	2
Alice Henson	Back St.	86	4
Mary Perrin	Naseby Lodge	84	3
Elisha Ringrose	Back St.	72	2
John Billing	Front St.	36	1
Robert Falkner	Front St.	30	1
	Totals:	3375	88

As we have already noticed all but seven of the farms were — three decades after enclosure — still in the village. The majority of the farmers were born in or around Naseby, the only exceptions being one from Suffolk and one from Rushden, Northants. The average size of the farms in 1851 was 136 acres.

The list of shopkeepers, traders and master craftsmen was made up of two licensed victuallers and a beer retailer, three carriers, a miller, a grocer, two butchers, and baker-and-draper, a general dealer, 8 carpenters, 6 blacksmiths, 13 shoemakers, 3 dressmakers and 3 tailors, 3 wheelwrights, a builder, a bricklayer and a brick-maker, a saddler, a basket maker. There was also a schoolmaster and a school mistress who were man and wife.

The working-class population of Naseby was composed of some 172 farm workers, 47 lace runners (mostly women), 31 servants, one errand boy and a traction engine driver. Of the labourers 167 were general farm workers. About 83 were in regular employment; the others were probably day-labourers. The remaining five were a shepherd, a groom, a gamekeeper, and two gardeners.

By 1871 the population had fallen by almost a fifth. The 177 households had been reduced to 166, and there had been a fall in the average size of household from 4.8 in 1851 to 4.1 in 1871. The most interesting change is the considerable redistribution of the landholding pattern amongst the tenant farmers. As figure 3 shows the total number of tenants had dropped from 22 to 14 (excluding those with a very small acreage and the graziers) but this, it seems, had not been the larger ones getting more prosperous at the expense of the smaller, since the average acreage had risen from 136 in 1851 to 216 in 1871. The large farm of Joseph Bassett in 1851 had been divided by 1871, and there had also been a reduction in the acreage of Woolleys Lodge from 290 acres to 160, but many of the smaller farms such as Broadmoor, John Smeeton's and Perrins', had grown in size. There had obviously not been a big influx of farmers in the twenty years since 1851 because only four of the fourteen names in 1871 were new ones. The rise of the Everards is noticeable. In 1851 they occupied two farms totalling 401 acres; by 1871 they had four farms and 1026 acres. By 1871 most of the farms had been moved out of the village, completing the intentions of the enclosure act.

Figure 3   *Farmers in 1871*

Farmer	Address	Acre-age	Employees Men	Boys
Thomas Colpman	Grange	326	8	6
Henry King	Manor Farm	305	9	4
David Everard	Broadmoor	290	5	1
John Smeeton	Cromwell House	290	5	3
Thomas Everard	Oak Lodge	265	6	3
John Everard	Vale	264	5	3
Thomas Watts and Nephew	Watts (Mill Hill)	260	6	4
Edward Varnam	—	220	6	3
George Everard	—	207	3	1
Mary Perrin	Perrins Lodge	195	4	2
Joseph Haddon	Fulbrook	167	4	1
Joseph Gilbert	Woolleys	160	3	2
John Ilston	Ilston's Lodge (Red Hill)	150	2	1
Benjamin White	Royal Oak	102	2	—
Jeremiah Wilford	—	37	1	1
Job Wilford, Grazier	—	11	2	—
John Everard, Grazier	—	5	—	—
Total Acreage		3254		
Employees			71	35

The number of agricultural labourers had fallen from 172 to 141 and the change was most marked with regard to the day-labourers whose numbers had dropped from 84 to less than 40. At the same time there had been an increase in the number of full-time farm employees from 88 in 1851 to 106 in 1871.

This undoubtedly marked an improvement in the position of the agricultural worker, making his work more regular, his labour scarcer and hence putting up its price. One consequence of this in the next few years was the rise of an active branch of Joseph Arch's National Agricultural Labourers Union in Naseby.

Since 1851 the lacemaking industry in the village had declined, the numbers having dropped from 47 to 18, and there were now only 3 smiths where there had been 6 in 1851. The wheelwrights had declined from 6 to 2, and there were now only 4 shoemakers where there had been 13 in 1851. Naseby was not destined to become a boot and shoe village. The number of shop-keepers had not altered significantly, but law and order now had a physical presence in the form of P.C. Edmund Stanton.

And finally the squire was now in his manor house. Shortly after his marriage in 1855 Captain George Ashby Maddock changed his name to George Ashby Ashby, and moved into Naseby Woolleys. He lived there, the dominant figure in the village, until he went bankrupt in 1887.

Since the 1870s the population of Naseby has declined steadily decade by decade for a century and it is only now in the 1970s that it is beginning to grow again.

Church, Chapel and Education in Victorian Naseby

Until 1825 the Church of England had a religious monopoly in Naseby. This was not accidental. In this closed village the landowners supported church control of religious provision and education and allowed no place of dissenting worship to be erected. Naseby dissenters had perforce to worship elsewhere.

The early history of Wesleyanism in the village is obscure and no account of its coming survives. It is probable that it was brought from Market Harborough, seven miles away. Methodism there goes back to 1776, and resulted from visits from John Wesley in 1741 and 1744. The earliest mention of Dissent in Naseby is that made by Mastin who claimed that the Friendly Society in 1792 was the cause of 'many sectaries . . . coming over to the Church'.[31] The Account Book of the Market Harborough Methodist Circuit Stewards (1814-1833) shows that there was a Methodist Society apparently flourishing in Naseby from 1814 at least, paying its quarterly contributions to circuit funds. Until 1825 these payments were on the small side, but from that year Naseby became, with Market Harborough, the largest contributor to circuit funds.[32] This was no doubt because the building of the chapel in 1825 swelled the ranks of the Methodists in the village.

In 1824 a letter was sent to John Purcell Fitzgerald making a request for a piece of land on which to build a chapel. This letter, in the form of a petition, stated that the undersigned considered that a chapel in addition to the parish church would be 'the means of promoting the temporal and spiritual welfare of many of the inhabitants of this populous village'.[33] It was signed by forty-six people including fourteen of the twenty-one farmers. Evidently Fitzgerald obliged, and in 1825 the chapel was erected.

In the next half-century Methodism flourished. In 1877 the vicar in his returns to the bishop stated that threequarters of the population were dissenters, adding the comment that their dissent was more political than religious. In the 1882 return the vicar declared that 'Dissent would count 4 to 1 Churchmen'.[34] The chapel was the focus of opposition to squire and parson in the village and it seems to have attracted farmers and labourers alike. When a conveyance of the chapel to new trustees was made in 1885, out of the twenty four trustees seven were farmers, four were labourers, and nine artisans. In 1871 it had been enlarged and restored; in 1876 was registered for the solemnisation of marriage; and in 1902 a new Sunday School was built. The strength of dissent in the village is undoubtedly one of the reasons for the support for Liberalism which manifested itself in Naseby in the last third of the century, and it might well have been a factor in the rise of the agricultural labourers' trade union after 1872.

The strength of the Methodists and the modesty of his stipend placed the vicar in Victorian Naseby in a position of some disadvantage, and were perhaps reasons for the fairly rapid succession of incumbents, (Between 1861 and 1895 there were seven vicars, an average length of residence of only five years). In 1849 the living was valued at only £84 per annum, despite having had an augmentation of £800 from Queen Anne's Bounty (with which thirty acres of land had been purchased in Long Buckby). This meant that the vicar had few resources to counter the Wesleyans. It was true that the landowners could be called upon for support, but the principal proprietor resided elsewhere and was rather remote. On the other hand Captain George Ashby Ashby gave the vicar and the church continuous support in his capacity of churchwarden from 1855 to 1887.

The Churchwardens of Naseby had twelve acres of land and ten cottages which they let each year, the rent providing them with a modest income out of which to pay for minor items of repair and upkeep of the church. But in 1858 it had become clear that the church was in want of major restoration. In addition to the nave needing repair the tower had become dangerous and needed completely rebuilding. The total cost proved to be £1,972 including £350 for the rebuilding of the tower and the addition of the graceful spire which now tops it. The dissenters opposed a church rate to meet the cost so the greater part of the money (some £1,340) was raised by subscriptions from far and near, and the sum needed for the tower and spire was borrowed from Lord Clifden and Captain Ashby, the church-wardens' land being mortgaged to make the repayments. An interesting point is that two thirds of the sum was borrowed from Lord Clifden and one third from Captain Ashby, strictly *pro rata*.[35] Another way money was raised was through the sale of souvenir postcards or (as the statement of accounts puts it) 'photographs of church by Rev. W. Law and others, done by Mr. Jennings of Market Harborough, after deducting the small price charged by the latter — £12.10.6.'.[36]

One (very English) way in which the church exerted a strong influence in this otherwise largely Methodist village was through the school. Although a school or schools were in existence in Naseby prior to the opening of the present one in 1843, little is known about the type of school or the degree of education that was offered. *The Select Committee on Education of the Poor* records that in 1818 there was in Naseby a school house erected 'about four years previously', wherein a Master instructed about forty-five children. Fifteen years later in 1833 the *Abstract of the Education Returns* shows that Naseby possessed 'one Infants School, containing about 60 children of both sexes, and one daily school, containing about 50 children'. From the copy of the conveyance of the land for the present school in Naseby, dated June 1844, it may be seen that the school itself and the teacher's house that we know today, were built shortly before this time. The land and buildings were given by the Fitzgerald family, and the curriculum to be taught in the school was set out, namely; reading, writing, arithmetic, geography, scripture, history, with needlework for the girls. Nothing has been discovered further about the school from this time until 1867, when the recording of school events in the Log Book commenced, throwing a great deal of light on village as well as school matters.[37]

Being a Church of England school, the links with the Church during the early years were very close. The school was subject to an annual inspection by the Diocesan Inspector, who examined the children in Religious Knowledge, and the original Fitzgerald deed of Conveyance stipulated that a certain number of hours each week must be set aside for religious instruction to be given by the Vicar, and to this day the vicar has the option of doing this if he so desires. The children of the Wesleyans were exempted from learning the catechism, and this affected about threequarters of the children attending the school. These children were required to bring notes from their parents stating that they did not wish them to receive instruction in the Church catechism, but this requirement was apparently effective only from 1895 onwards. The vicar was a frequent visitor to the school, for in addition to giving religious instruction in his capacity of school manager, he also checked the registers and examined the children in subjects other than catechism.

In 1870, three years after the Log Book commenced, school attendance officers were appointed under the Education Act, and great emphasis was now laid on regular attendance. The work of the attendance officer was of great importance, because from 1862 until the 1890s the amount of Government grant which a school and its teachers earned depended on regular attendance and on children passing the set standards. Despite the efforts of the Attendance Officer, many children were consistently absent from school: at times this led to parents being fined at the Northampton Magistrates' Court. Several factors were found to affect the attendance rate throughout the year, for instance many children stayed away from school simply to help with work at home or in the village, and it seems little notice was taken of the frequent warnings issued by the Attendance Officer. The situation was not improved by the practice of local tradesmen employing children of school age to assist in their businesses. There was no real improvement in this situation until July 1891 when a Naseby farmer was fined 10/-d. with 18/6d. costs for employing children of school age.

From 1870 the managers were most anxious to keep up the village school and avoid the imposition of a non-sectarian Board School (which would

OLD COB COTTAGES IN NASEBY
(Photograph: Northampton Public Library)

also have had to be paid for out of the rates) as the following letter to the firm of Fisher and Saunders, Land Agents of Market Harborough, shows. (The firm was administering the estate of Captain Ashby after his bankruptcy in 1887.)

'Dear sir,

Being Parish Churchwarden for Naseby and the responsible Manager of the National Day School and having to provide funds to carry it on, I write to ask you if you will give us an annual subscription (As Landlord). Our School is carried on by voluntary subscription and we want to keep it up and so keep out a School Board. This we should not be able to do if it were not for Lord Clifton's [sic] subscription of £25 per year. We hope other Landlords will help also. Captain Ashby used to subscribe £10 annually and we feel the loss of his subscription.'[38]

It is not known whether Fisher and Saunders, as surrogate squires, made a contribution.

Between the years 1867 and 1876 Naseby school saw a rather rapid turnover in masters and mistresses, there being four in nine years. It is not clear why, though relationships with the vicars probably had much to do with it. In 1876, however, a Mr. Houghton began a fourteen year residence in the school house. He was a respected figure and when he and his wife were abruptly dismissed in 1890 he printed a sheet of verses as a 'Letter of farewell'.[39] It illustrates some of the problems of the village schoolmaster in the years after Forster's Education Act.

> 'On the eve
> Of vanishing and taking leave
> Of you and Naseby, it occurs
> To me to notice some few slurs
> And calumnies in the air'

He denies the charge of incompetency, and lists the government grant the school had earned each year under his mastership. He went on

> 'I do not overlook
> The fact that for the present year
> A falling-off will there appear,
> But, please remember, as a fine
> Two-thirds of the Five Pounds' loss was mine
> And, you should also bear in mind
> That illness threw us much behind,
> For "influenza" played its part
> Just when the children wanted "heart"
> The average — on which *all* is paid —
> Became reduced, we miss its aid'

And he instances other hazards to the schoolmaster of the 'payment by results' system.

> 'Then our Examiner was new
> And "failed" the very best, a few
> Of whom for certain one can tell
> They do their work and do it well;
> And "Grammar" (not our weakest point)
> Was butchered — hackled — joint by joint;
> Yet, when the tell-tale schedules came
> *I* only had to shoulder blame:
> Whereas School Guardians ought to dare
> To challenge what appears unfair
>   If after passing hundreds through
> (With twenty-one years' service too!)
> I am to be belied and spurned;
> I think my triumphs dearly earned'

Houghton was succeeded by a Mr. Bartlett who (not so easily moved) toiled in Naseby for 35 years, coming into the living memory of present villagers. The master was invariably assisted by his wife, who taught the infants, and needlework to the girls. From the 1890s it became common practice for paid monitors and pupil teachers to help with the teaching. These monitors were usually ex-pupils, and if they so desired could continue through the stages of probationary teacher, temporary teacher, articled teacher, until they teached their final goal and became certificated.

A steady increase in the number of pupils was recorded up until the period 1890-95, when a peak of 126 was reached, and from 1900 to 1912 there was a steady decline in numbers settling down at about 70 pupils from 1915 to the end of the period covered by the Log Books (1928).

The school had four main holidays each year. The Christmas and Easter holidays lasted for approximately two weeks each and in June another week was given for the Naseby feast and Rothwell Fair. It was realised that unless a holiday was given for the Fair, many children would be absent from school anyway. Even so in the week preceding attendances were often very low as many children were kept at home to help with the preparations for what was the great event in the year. The longest holiday was in summer, and usually lasted for five weeks. The start of it coincided with the harvest time, the tradition being that school broke up as soon as one field had been 'carried'. Since harvest varied each year — from the end of June (1868) to early September (1871) — so therefore did the timing of the holiday. A marked falling off in attendance was always noted in the week preceding the holiday as the harvesting activities got under way and pupils stayed away from school in order to help parents and farmers. In the early summer many children helped with hay-making or with willow peeling at the basket makers instead of attending school. It is interesting to note that the working of the Education Act was suspended for the duration of the five weeks holiday so that the children could legally help with the harvest, but many children continued to stay away after the holiday and ended, in order to help with other jobs such as gleaning and potato raising. This sometimes resulted in the new term being postponed for a further week. In addition, Naseby children helped with any jobs which demanded casual labour throughout the year, beansetting, bird scaring, potato setting and gardening, with attendance at school always taking second place!

The school played an important role in the day-to-day life of the village, being in many ways the forerunner of the present village hall. Evening activities took place there; one of the earliest to be recorded in the Log Books was the 'Penny Readings', where people from the village, on payment of the sum of 1d. could listen to readings from books by contemporary authors. Concerts were held in the school rooms, at which the children occasionally took part, or wrote the programmes. An annual event was the church choir concert and supper; and others included Temperance meetings, church missions, may day festivities, kine shows, political meetings, dances, whist drives, magic lantern exhibitions, conjurers and even, in September 1906, Bill Bailey's Variety Company! And once a year, in November, there was the Annual Provident Clothing Club Sale, which caused the school to be closed for the day.

The Log Book records the customs observed by the children, the most notable being May Day. A school holiday was usually given for the occasion, and the girls paraded garlands through the village and danced around the maypole. Festivities were held in the school room in the evening, which culminated in the crowning of the May Queen. A half day holiday was always given for Shrove Tuesday. In 1885 several of the children enacted the old custom of 'barring out' by taking possession of the school before it opened. All doors were locked and barricaded and an enraged schoolmaster had to gain entry through one of the windows. Ash Wednesday and Holy Thursday were observed by the children attending a morning service in the church. Certain other customs were recorded in the Log Books, among those of interest is Oak Apple Day, held on May 29th, and was observed by all the children wearing sprigs of Oak, and similarly on April 20th, Primrose Day was observed. One reference is also made to Plough Monday on January 13th, but no details are given. It was also customary for the school children to have a few hours off school to observe the first meet of the season of the Pytchley Hunt in Naseby. On one occasion considerable excitement was caused within the school when a fox being pursued by the Pytchley sought sanctuary within the school building. It was eventually ejected and its brush was later presented to the schoolmistress and mask to the school.

Naseby schoolchildren also had holidays to celebrate national events like Queen Victoria's Jubilee, and Coronation Weeks in 1902 and 1911. One day's holiday was granted in 1913 to mark the occasion of the visit of King George V to Northampton, and in 1919 one week was added to the summer holidays to commemorate the signing of the Peace Treaty.

Working Class Naseby

The social history of the agricultural labourers who formed the greater part of the population of nineteenth century Naseby is largely lost. Scattered pieces of information only remain. The historian of temperance in Northamptonshire noted (in 1898) that in the 1840s a Mr. Wykes had lent his barn for meetings at Naseby, but no Temperance Association seems to have been formed.[40] In 1862 a co-operative grocery stores had been started and by 1872 had a membership of 35. But it seems to have failed thereafter.

In 1873 the Naseby labourers established a branch of Joseph Arch's National Agricultural Labourers' Union.[41] Although the Union eventually collapsed it generated a democratic impulse and an urge for 'self-help' which was not suppressed. In Naseby as elsewhere the Union was frowned upon by those in authority. One small example of this is to be found in the Account Book of the Naseby Coal Club. This was a provident body of which Captain Ashby was both patron and honorary treasurer. Most families were subscribers and the farmers played their part by carrying the coal free of charge from the canal wharf at Welford. In 1873 51 members were suddenly paid out, most of them on 28 April. No explanation was given of this save a note against the name of Thomas Halford in December: he 'ought not to have had coal as he had joined the Union, but did not come and draw his money out like the other men on joining'.[42] It is not clear whether there was a wholesale dismissal of the union men, or a mass walk-out from a squirearchial charity. It seems from the note that it was the former.

Arch's union was eventually broken nationally by lock-outs. Evidence of this in Naseby is seen in the school log-book which shows that in 1874 many of the older boys were absent from school to help with field work during this 'strike'. However, the movement did not collapse. 1874 saw the first great union demonstration in the parish, at which 220 people sat down to tea in a large booth erected by the landlord of the Fitzgerald Arms, who was a friend of the Union. It was realised by Arch and his followers that there was propaganda value in meeting in Naseby, on the site of the battle in which traditional authority had sustained such a grievous blow, and the next year the demonstration was held on June 14, the day of the battle. Some 2,000 people attended to hear Arch, and so sign petitions in favour of the extension of the franchise to the agricultural workers and against the Game Laws, and sing Union songs. To the reporter from the *Northampton Mercury* 'The village presented a decided holiday appearance, bands of music paraded the streets, and well dressed men and women with hats, bonnets or coats decorated with blue rosettes, were to be seen everywhere. From an early hour the labourers from the surrounding villages flooded into Naseby, and about noon a procession was formed, headed by the Northampton Town Band . . . and a Guilsborough band. With banners unfurled, the party marched as far as the obelisk erected to commemorate the battle, and there stationed themselves until the arrival of their leader, Mr. Arch, and his friends, from Market Harborough'.[43] In the years 1876 to 1880 similar demonstrations were held, bringing crowds of people into the village.

One by-product of the Union was the founding of a Friendly Society to provide sickness benefits, medical aid and funeral benefits. What was unusual about it was that it was registered as a separate entity with the Chief Registrar of Friendly Societies. By the end of 1877 it had a membership of 44, and it survived another twenty years, even though the Labourers' Union had been dead for over ten years elsewhere in Northamptonshire by then.[44] The Union 'club', however, was not the only one founded in Naseby at this time. In April 1874 Court 'Cromwell Victory', a branch of the Ancient Order of Forresters was started, to rival the old-established Oddfellows Lodge in the village, which did not admit labourers.

The union stimulated working-class politics in Naseby. In 1875 the branch sent its own representatives to a franchise demonstration in London, and in 1877, when Liberal Party activity in the county revived when Gladstone came back into politics over the Russo-Turkish war, Arch spoke on the subject at the great Naseby rally in June. In 1882 204 Naseby people signed a petition to Parliament in favour of the proposed Allotments Extension Act. And in 1886 at a meeting of the Union branch a resolution was passed supporting Gladstone's policy of Home Rule for Ireland.[45]

The value of Naseby and its Civil War associations as anti-conservative propaganda was also recognized by the Nonconformists who were an important part of Northamptonshire Liberalism in the eighties and nineties. On 15 June 1899 the county Nonconformists, emulating the labourers' Union, met to celebrate the anniversary of the battle.[46] In 1901 the Naseby Cromwell Library was opened to commemorate the tercentenary of the Lord Protector's birth. Among the subscribers were Earl Spencer, Mr. J. H. Smeeton of Oak Lodge, a Baptist farmer, and the Baptist minister of Long

Buckby, a prominent Liberal. The Library (which is still preserved) is an interesting collection of books and pamphlets on the battle and the Civil War.

The granting of the vote to the rural labourers in 1885 was followed by the introduction for the first time of representative parish government in 1894. At the first parish council election the old order in the village in the persons of the churchwardens was swept from power, and a nine-man council consisting of three farmers, three agricultural workers and three others were returned. The old order did not go gracefully. When the parish councillors sought to carry out one of their first duties, to take possession of the parish records, there was reluctance on the part of the church-wardens to part with the sturdily bound enclosure award which led to an undignified struggle in the church, an account of which appeared in the local paper fifty years later under the inevitable headline 'The Second Battle of Naseby is Recalled'.[47]

Modern Naseby

The population decline which started in the middle of the nineteenth century has continued into our own times. By 1971 the population of Naseby had shrunk to no more than 350.

This process was part of the general drift from the land from 1850 which was a national rather than a local phenomenon. Migration was quickened by the depression in agriculture in the 1870s and 1880s. In Naseby the depression's most noteable victim was Captain George Ashby Ashby, who went bankrupt in 1887, in the words of the Official Receiver, because of 'continual losses in farming over a period of 13 years'. One of the chief secured creditors was the Land Improvement Company, and it is clear that Ashby had tried to be too much of a model landlord at a time when land values and profits were on the decline.[48] He may also have been extravagant: village legend has it that the teeth of his dogs were capped with gold. Part of the 'Ashby inheritance' — the mansion with a hundred acres, and four farms — was put up for sale passing to a Major Munday — whilst the rest was managed by the land agents, Fisher and Saunders, of Market Harborough. Eventually the whole of the Ashby estate consisting of 1053 acres was sold to Major Renton in 1904. About that time the other Naseby estate had changed hands too. The trustees of Viscount Clifden had sold it to Lord Annaly of Holdenby, who became lord of the manor as well as chief landowner.

It was the agricultural depression of the eighteen eighties rather than the enclosure act which led to the end of the old community of Naseby. As a result of it many of the old Naseby families had gone by the end of the century; the passing of the Everards, who had been in Naseby since the mid-seventeenth century at least and who in 1871 tenanted five farms, and the passing of the Adnitts, of whom there were fifteen family groups in 1871, being examples. Today there are in Naseby only eight family names out of the sixty four recorded in 1871. This depression made way for an influx of farmers from other parts of the country, principally the hill and marginal farming areas of the south-west and Wales, and it is the descendants of these 'newcomers' who farm much of the parish in 1973. They came because what to them was good land had crashed in value; they came too because they were accustomed to hard living, whereas the old Naseby families had grown comfortable and the decline of their circumstances was more than they could take.

The depression, which more than anything else brought about the passing of the 'old order' in Naseby, only really lifted with the start of the first World War and the consequent need throughout the country for greater food production. From 1914, many acres of pasture disappeared under plough, and more cereals and root crops were grown. The traditional mixed farm still existed however with beef and dairy cattle, sheep, pigs, poultry and arable side by side — the age of specialisation was still nearly half a century away.

But the temporary improvement in farming which the war brought was short lived. The Naseby men who returned from the forces were soon in a situation only too similar to what they had known before they left. In the 1920s and 1930s the land in the parish became more neglected than it had been for many years, and the whole landscape took on an appearance of disuse. Hedges grew tall, fields were allowed to slip back to pasture and became full of anthills. It was said that 'there was hardly a ploughed field to be seen between here and Leicester'. Farming progressed only with the introduction of mechanisation; the first tractors and lorries appeared in the 1930s, but before this there had been steam engines to help with the ploughing. One engine was stationed at each end of the field and the plough run on a winch between them, with the ploughman only keeping it level. There were then only two threshing machines in the village, which were taken round the farms in turn. Crops at this time were grown chiefly for farm feed — oats for the horses and barley for the pigs.

Once again it was war that brought about a revival in 1939. Mechanisation increased its pace, and ploughing started again, under the sometimes incomprehensible direction of the 'War Ag.' Ministry in London. Some flax was grown, pulled by hand, stacked and carted to the Flax Mills at Billing. The quality was suitable for rough cloth only and the crop went out of fashion and the mill closed soon after the war was over, but it had had the beneficial side-effect of cleansing the soil of the wireworm which had previously infested it. Other crops to make their appearance (or re-appearance) in the war years were potatoes (also hand harvested), sugar beet, and on a small acreage, linseed. Amongst villagers allotments started again in earnest, under the 'Dig for Victory' campaign, and the 'cottager's pig' also re-appeared; a club was formed for the purpose of bulk buying of feed, and the ancient art of pig curing was brought back by the few who could remember it. Another old practice to start up again was that of gleaning, with the particular object of getting feed for the backyard poultry. The 'War Ag.' also had the power to dispossess farmers, and one Naseby tenant had a yearly tenancy terminated under these powers.

Naseby knew the same war experiences as most other rural areas. It had its Home Guard Unit, A.R.P., St. John's, Firewatchers, and, not least, the Women's Land Army. Irish labourers were 'imported' and the hostel built for them was also used successively by the Land Girls and by Prisoners of War. Evacuee children came from the East End of London (and soon went home again); Naseby Woolleys was occupied by the Yorkshire Insurance Company; and a stick of bombs even fell as near as three miles away.

If depression after the second war was avoided, changes in farming were nevertheless slow. The first combine harvesters came about 1950, the early models were 'Baggers' which required a three man crew of driver, bed leveller and bag handler. Until the 1950s, farming was still truly mixed, but then specialisation started, with new breeds of cattle and sheep replacing traditional 'all-purpose' breeds, and farmers began to concentrate on arable or cattle or sheep. Free-range pigs and poultry disappeared from the farms at about this time. Towards the end of the 1960s new crops began to appear, the bright yellow flower of the rape making a dramatic change to the early summer field colours and new technologies were pioneered such as direct drilling and minimal cultivation, earlier than in many other places. Land prices followed the rocketing national pattern, as did the prices for meat and corn in the early years of the 1970s.

The village itself had changed little after the rebuilding of the 1870s and 1880s, when the new labourers' cottages, built in red brick to replace the old mud-walled dwellings, attracted favourable comment from the Royal Commission on Labour in 1894. One or two private houses were built, and in the 1930s ten council houses, to be followed by a further four after the war. But the building boom which hit many Northamptonshire villages situated closer to main roads or towns missed Naseby until the late 1960s. Then between 1969 and 1972 nearly 30 new private houses were built and this would seem to be the beginning of a still greater growth. It has brought into Naseby for the first time in its history a new class of people, the urban commuter, and undoubtedly heralds a completely new period in the history of this (and many another) ancient midland village.

LIST OF REFERENCES

Abbreviations: NRO, Northamptonshire Record Office; PRO, Public Record Office.

1. T. Carlyle *Oliver Cromwell's Letters and Speeches*, 1845, Letter XXIX.
2. W. F. Grimes 'The Jurassic Way Across England' in *Aspects of Archaeology. Essays presented to O. G. S. Crawford*, 1951, pp. 144-171.
3. J. E. B. Gover, A. Mawer and F. M. Stenton *Place Names of Northamptonshire*, 1933, p. 73.
4. G. Joan Fuller 'Settlement in Northamptonshire between 500 AD and the Domesday', *East Midland Geographer*, 1955, Vol. 3, pp. 25-36.
5. There are 24 charters in the *Add. MSS.*, British Museum.
6. *Calendar of Close Rolls 1237-42*, p. 38.
7. *Calendar of Inquisitions Post Mortem*, IX, p. 54.
8. *ibid.*
9. NRO. S.S. 3751.
10. PRO E179/155/28. Microfilm at NRO.
11. J. C. Russell *British Medieval Population*, Albaquerque, 1948, p. 23.
12. At NRO.
13. The Compton Return for Northamptonshire is in print in *Northamptonshire Antiquarian Memoranda*, XXVII, 'Church and Dissent in 1676'.
14. PRO 179/254/14. Microfilm copy at NRO.
15. (ed.) V. A. Hatley *Northamptonshire Militia Lists 1777*, 1973, p. 71.
16. J. Mastin *History and Antiquities of Naseby*, 1792, p. 22.
17. *ibid.*, pp. 15-16.
18. *ibid.*, p. 16.
19. *ibid.*, pp. 17-18.
20. *ibid.*, pp. 18-19.
21. *ibid.*, p. 21.
22. *ibid.*, pp. 50-1.
23. *ibid.*, p. 51.
24. *ibid.*, pp. 51-2.
25. *ibid.*, pp. 78-9.
26. NRO *Fisher and Saunders papers*. Bankruptcy of Capt. Ashby.
27. Ipswich and East Suffolk Record Office. *Purcell Fitzgerald Papers*, Box 30.
28. NRO *Court Rolls and Court Book of the Manor of Naseby 1803-1825*.
29. Information from Endor Halford Esq.
30. PRO HO.107/1742 and RG.10/1494.
31. Mastin *History and Antiquities of Naseby*, p. 79.
32. Leicestershire County Record Office. *Account Book of the Market Harborough Wesleyan Methodist Circuit Stewards 1814-1833*.
33. *Market Harborough Methodist Circuit Papers* (in the keeping of the Rev. Victor Martin, Market Harborough).
34. NRO *Diocesan Records. Bishops' Visitations*, 1877 and 1882.
35. Naseby Parish Records. *MS Minute Book of the Parish Vestry, 1849-1931*.
36. Naseby Parish Records. *Statement of Accounts of Church Restoration*.
37. In the possession of the headmaster, Naseby Infants and Primary School.
38. NRO *Fisher and Saunders Papers* Box 1.

39. Broadsheet. In the possession of Endor Halford Esq.

40. Frank Bates *Lights and Landmarks of the Temperance Movement in Northampton-shire,* 1898, p. 10.

41. This section is largely based on Pamela Horn's 'Nineteenth Century Naseby Farm Workers' in *Northamptonshire Past and Present,* IV, 1968-9, pp. 167-173.

42. Naseby Parish Records. *MS Book of Naseby Coal Club 1870-1887.*

43. *Northampton Mercury* 19 June 1875.

44. Pamela Horn *Naseby Farm Workers* op. cit.

45. *ibid.*

46. *Northampton Mercury* 12 March 1909.

47. *Market Harborough Advertiser and Midland Mail* 16 May 1947.

48. NRO *Fisher and Saunders Papers* Box 1.